The Mind of Christ

The Mind of Christ

DENNIS F. KINLAW

FRANCIS ASBURY PRESS
of Evangel Publishing House

Nappanee, Indiana 46550

THE MIND OF CHRIST
Copyright © 1998 by The Francis Asbury Society
P.O. Box 7, Wilmore, Kentucky 40390

Requests for information should be addressed to:
Evangel Publishing House
2000 Evangel Way
P.O. Box 189
Nappanee, Indiana 46550
Phone: (800) 253-9315
Internet: www.evangelpublishing.com

Edited by Joseph D. Allison
Cover Design by Foster & Foster

ISBN: 0-916035-93-X
Library of Congress Catalog Card Number: 98-072659

Printed in the United States of America

9 0 1 2 3 4 EP 10 9 8 7 6 5 4 3

CONTENTS

PREFACE

Martin Luther said that the sword of the Spirit is sheathed in the languages. He set himself to the task of learning Latin, Greek, and Hebrew so that he could understand the Scriptures in the languages of their earliest expression. Roman Catholic authorities were scandalized when Luther translated the Bible into the popular German of his day; yet he knew that the Word of God had to be put into fresh terms, so that people could read God's revealed truth in terms they could understand.

Over the years, I have been privileged to study the biblical languages with some of the brightest scholars of our time. Linguists get very excited about their work. As I read the journal articles that pour from the presses each month, I thrill along with other biblical scholars at the new things being discovered. But not all new biblical insights come from esoteric scholarship. The Scriptures also can speak afresh to a heart that has been touched by the Spirit of God.

The little book that you hold in your hands is intended to accomplish two things: (1) Express the teachings of God's Word in terms that a modern reader can readily grasp. (2) Allow the Holy Spirit to show you the truth that has always been in God's Word. If these two goals can be accomplished, I believe the sword of the Spirit will be unsheathed to accomplish some marvelous things in your life.

Let me comment a bit further on my first objective, to express the Bible's teachings in contemporary terms. In the 1980s, I interviewed for a faculty position a bright young woman whose father had written a classic introductory textbook on theology. His name is not well-known today, but he held a sacred place in my memory because I had used his book to teach several classes in my early academic days. His daughter was extremely intelligent and articulate. She impressed me as being a very capable scholar in her own right. As the interview drew to a close, I could restrain my curiosity no longer. I leaned forward in my chair and said, "What can you tell me about your father?"

A benign smile crossed the young lady's face. "Well," she said, "his terminology was rather simplistic, wasn't it?"

I thought, *This young lady has earned her Ph.D., so now she's looking down her nose at her father.*

"Let me ask you a question," I said. "Don't you think that the vocabulary we believe is so sophisticated today will seem simplistic to students thirty years from now?"

She burst into tears. I was surprised that my question had drawn such a response. As she hurriedly excused herself from my office, I thought, *She has distanced herself from her spiritual heritage and her only reason is, "It's too simplistic."*

Our generation rejects many truths of God simply because we have linked those truths to the doctrinal terminology of our parents, grandparents, or great-grandparents. Terms like "personal holiness," "entire sanctification," "the second blessing," and "the baptism of the Holy Spirit" are rejected out of hand, because they were common currency at the turn of the century. Yet the truth behind those terms is still central to God's Word. We short-change ourselves if we ignore what God teaches us, simply because we feel uncomfortable with the language that has been used to express it over the years.

This is why I believe that biblical exegesis has to be re-done every fifty years or so. Not only is our understanding of theology continually changing. Our language is continually changing, too. The words that struck fire in the imagination of our grandparents may seem like soggy matches today. We need to find what the Bible is actually saying at these points, then put it into fresh words that our own generation can comprehend. That's my first objective here.

Secondly, I hope this book will be a tool that the Holy Spirit can use to open your eyes to the truth of God's Word. The Holy Spirit inspires each stage of the communication process through which the Scriptures have come to us. He inspired the original writers; he inspires each new generation of translators; and he continues to inspire the people who read the Bible, day by day. The Holy Spirit speaks at every stage of the process, so that God's truth can be revealed. If this book can bring you into a life-changing encounter with the Lord, the Spirit will have a new opportunity to open God's Word to you.

This book explores how common people such as you and I can have the mind of Christ. The mind of Christ is not a closely-guarded secret; his thinking is on open display throughout the Bible. Yet the mind of Christ is a forgotten theme in modern theology. After you become aware of how our Lord thinks, you will be surprised to see how often it emerges in the Scriptures and in the most unexpected places.

I believe that if you come to this book with a teachable heart, it can transform your life. I say that, not out of vain pride as an author, but out of the recognition that God has changed thousands of people's lives when they grasped their need to have the mind of Christ.

I pray that the Holy Spirit will unsheathe his sword and pierce your heart as you read this book. May he convince you to become a person who thinks as Christ thinks, a person who lives as Christ lives.

Dennis F. Kinlaw

1

The Forgotten Theme

I have a friend who loves to fly small airplanes. One day, he suggested that I might like to take a ride with him. I said, "I would love to." So I found myself sitting in the cockpit of this little plane made for two people. I was bewildered by the array of instruments in front of us, but he said, "Dennis, there are two instruments that you must have in any plane, no matter how big or small."

I don't know much about piloting airplanes, so I asked, "What are those?"

"One of them is the compass," he said, pointing to it.

"What is the other one?"

"The other is an artificial horizon." He pointed to an odd-looking electronic dial on the dash. I saw a line across the dial, which was thicker at each end.

"Harry, why do you need an artificial horizon?"

"It tells you the difference between 'up' and 'down,'" he replied.

I thought he was trying to play a practical joke on me, and I was not about to be snookered. I said, "Harry, are you so stupid that you can't tell the difference between 'up' and 'down'?"

He looked at me with a mischievous grin and said, "Kinlaw, I'm not the stupid one. When we get into the clouds and cannot see anything outside of the plane, nothing in our bodies will tell us which way is 'up' and which way is 'down.' When we rise into that cloud cover, I have just a few seconds to get adjusted to using that artificial horizon, because my body will tell me one thing, but reality will be something else."

Another friend of mine was a jet pilot in the Korean War. One of his companions crashed his plane at full speed straight into the ground beside a freight train, because he thought the red light on the end of the freight train was the wingtip light of his buddy flying next to him.

We have no artificial horizon inside of us. We have no internal compass. Our bodies bear witness to the fact that we need guidance from outside of ourselves. Yet so often we think, *It's my life. I can control it. I don't need God or anyone else.* Then we make great mistakes, damaging our own lives and the lives of other people.

The prophet Jeremiah says our way is not in us; it is in the Lord (Jer. 10:23). More than anything else in my life, I need the guidance of the Lord. I need him, not just to save me and forgive my sins, but I need him to live with me all the time. I need him every minute of every day, because if I lose my connection with him, I lose my way. That's why Jesus said, "I am the Way" (John 14:6). I believe he was not speaking metaphorically, but very literally and practically.

This is also the reason God has given us the Scriptures. He meant the Scriptures to be a great gift. The Word of God is not a burden that he wants to impose on us; the Bible helps us find out who we are supposed to be and how we are to live. So the more we know about it, the safer we are. The more we know about it, the richer we are.

Take a closer look at the passage from Jeremiah that I mentioned a moment ago. He says, "I know, O Lord, that the way of human beings is not in their control, that mortals as they walk cannot direct their steps" (Jer. 10:23). The Hebrew word translated here as "human beings" is *adam;* it refers to the entirety of the human race. Jeremiah says this statement applies to every human being who has ever lived or ever will live. None of us can control our way by ourselves. In the second half of the verse, Jeremiah uses the Hebrew word *ish,* which the NRSV translates as "mortals." This word refers to individuals. He's saying that what is true of humanity's general destiny is true of each one of us in our daily living. We cannot direct our steps; we cannot find our way alone.

That expression, "direct their steps" (or, "find their way"), is a Semitic idiom for goal-orientedness. Striving to achieve goals is a basic characteristic of every human being. Each of us wants to get somewhere. That's why, if you are driving an automobile in an unfamiliar town, you hate to get lost on dead-end streets. You are going somewhere in particular and you don't want to be delayed. Every human being has an innate sense that he or she is supposed to accomplish something and achieve a goal.

Yet the prophet says our sense of direction is not in us. In no way can we achieve the goal we ought to achieve by ourselves. Jeremiah says that the only way we can achieve what we are supposed to achieve and reach the goals we are supposed to reach is if we know God, the true God, and we are rightly related to him.

As I have gotten older, I have come to the same conclusion. The greatest gift that God can give to any of us is an inner hunger for him. I find myself saying, "Lord, intensify my hunger for you. Get me to the place where the deepest passion of my being is for you. There is no safety anywhere else. There is nothing of value anywhere else."

Having "The Mind of Christ"

In this connection, the Scriptures talk a great deal about having the mind which was in Christ Jesus. These texts suggest that we can have a kind of internal guidance system, a bit like my friend Harry's artificial horizon, within our minds and hearts. The astonishing thing about this guidance system, though, is that it will enable us to walk like Jesus walks—to pursue the goals he pursues, with the attitudes and passions that Christ himself has. So I have become intensely interested in what the Bible had to say about having "the mind of Christ."

Many of these references appear in connection with the Greek verb *phroneō*, which occurs 29 times in the New Testament. *Phroneō* is tellingly used in Mark 8. There Jesus asks his disciples, "Who do you say that I am?" and Peter replies, "You are the Messiah" (v. 29). Jesus then tells them that he is about to suffer and die. "God forbid it, Lord!" Peter cries. "This must never happen to you" (Matt. 16:22). And Jesus says to him, "Get behind me, Satan! For you are setting your mind (Gk., *phroneis*) not on divine things but on human things" (Mark 8:33).

Another important text is found in Philippians, where we read, "Let the same mind be in you that was in Christ Jesus" (Phil. 2:5). The verb translated "let this mind" is *phroneō*. The verse could also be translated, "Have the same attitude toward one another as you have in Christ Jesus," or, "Be disposed toward one another as you are toward Christ Jesus." That verb *phroneō* suggests more than logic; it suggests an attitude.

Paul again uses that word significantly in Romans 8, where he says, "Those who live according to the flesh set their minds (Gk., *phronousin*) on the things of the flesh, but those who live according to the Spirit set their minds on the things of the Spirit" (v. 5). He is not merely talking about a philosophical system. The word suggests the desires of a person's heart. We get a similar connotation in Colossians 3:2-3, where Paul says, "Set your minds (Gk., *phroneite*) on things that are above, not on things that are on earth, for you have died, and your life is hidden with Christ in God."

We will return to these passages in more detail later in this book. At this point, I want you to notice that all of the texts I have mentioned do not point us toward a system of philosophy or a set of religious beliefs. They are not challenging us to live by a certain creed. To have "the mind of Christ" is to have his perspective, his attitude, his affections and priorities. The Bible calls us to have the mind of Christ within us, rather than merely learning how to imitate him. We are challenged to allow his mind to guide our lives. This is such a marvelous thing that we can scarcely comprehend it.

The Gospels challenge us to think the way Christ thinks. The New Testament Epistles emphasize that we should expect "the mind of Christ" to be given to us. This is not only a theme of the New Testament, however. The motif runs throughout the Old Testament as well, even though the phrase "the mind of Christ" does not appear there.

An Old Testament Theme

Consider Abram's attempt to get an heir through Hagar, his wife's servant (Gen. 15). Abram despaired of ever having his own son, but God promised, "Your very own issue shall be your heir" (v. 4). As the years rolled by, that promise seemed more and more incredible. So Abram and his wife Sarai took matters into their own hands. Abram conceived a son by Hagar and named the boy Ishmael; this was the beginning of bitter strife within Abram's family, which continues to this day. Abram's impulsive decision illustrates how even a devout man can fail to think as God thinks.

King Saul's blasphemy at the altar of Gilgal is another example (1 Sam. 13). God had chosen Saul to be the first king of Israel. Then Saul faced an overwhelming enemy force. Afraid that his people were leaving him, Saul offered a burnt sacrifice before the priest Samuel arrived. It was the expedient thing to do. Yet Samuel gravely told him that he had acted foolishly (v. 13). "Now your kingdom will not continue," the priest said, "the Lord has sought out a man after his own heart…" (v. 14).

The history of Israel's kings gives us a sad litany of such wayward thinking. For generations, the nation suffered under the foolish administration of men who followed their own instincts rather than the clear direction of the Lord.

Yet the Old Testament is not simply a record of failure on this score. "Enoch walked with God; then he was no more, for God took him" (Gen. 5:24). "…Noah was a righteous man, blameless in his generation; Noah walked with God" (Gen. 6:9). The prophet Elijah went walking with the Lord one day and ended up in heaven (2 Kings 2). King Hezekiah was able to say to the Lord, "…I have walked before you in faithfulness with a whole heart, and have done what is good in your sight" (Isa. 38:3). Clearly, the Old Testament demonstrates that servants of God can "walk" with him—i.e., share God's thoughts, affections, and goals, in intimate communion with him. (There's that Semitic idiom again!)

God declared through the prophet Ezekiel, "A new heart I will give you, and a new spirit I will put within you; and I will remove from your body the heart of stone and give you a heart of flesh. I will put my spirit within you, and make you follow my statutes and be careful to observe my ordinances" (Ezek. 36:26-27). Why would God promise such a radical change in his people, unless he planned to do it?

In the chapters to come, we will explore these passages and similar ones in greater depth. The point I wish to make here is simply this: *A major motif of Scripture is that God can enable his people to think as he thinks.* Yet this is a forgotten theme in modern evangelicalism.

Few Have Found It

The Bible calls us to have "the mind of Christ," yet the Bible also says it is relatively rare for people to think as Christ thinks. Two troubling Gospels make this clear. The first is the Gospel of John, which shows us that devout people do not instinctively have "the mind of Christ." Read what happened when Jesus drove the money changers out of the Temple (John 2:13-25).

The Temple authorities did not know who Jesus was. How under the sun could that have been possible? They had been waiting two thousand years for him. The purpose of the Temple in Jerusalem was to identify him when he came. The Temple was designed to be his house. Now when the President shows up at the White House after the inauguration, the servants don't say, "What are you doing here?" But that's what happened in the Temple (see John 2:18). Why did they miss him? Because he didn't come the way they thought he would come. Their paradigm of power was wrong.

The Temple authorities believed that the Messiah would come with spectacular displays of physical power. They expected him to be a strong military leader like Judas Maccabeus, or possibly a shrewd king like Solomon. They could not understand how a humble carpenter's son from Nazareth could be the Son of God. They could not believe that a sandaled man wearing a simple cotton robe and riding a lowly donkey could be the conqueror of the world. They could not accept that a friend of fishermen and tax collectors could teach them anything about how the Temple should be governed. The rulers of the Temple were devout men, but when it came to knowing the ways of God, they were wrong.

Jesus demonstrated that the ultimate authority in all creation is self-sacrificing. The center of absolute, ultimate, eternal authority is found in the broken, bleeding body of the eternal Son of God. Power is not what we humanly think it is; power is the ability to sacrifice yourself for someone other than yourself. Most of us miss this point.

The second troubling Gospel is that of Mark. While John demonstrates that Jesus' enemies don't think the way he does, Mark confronts us with the fact that even Jesus' best friends don't think the way he does. The first half of the Gospel of Mark consists of stories about Jesus. These stories recount either what he does or parables that he says, and are all designed to answer the question, "Who is this guy?" Then, after all others have expressed their opinions, Jesus turns to his disciples and asks, "But who do you say that I am?" Peter immediately says, "You are the Messiah" (Mark 8:29).

From that point, the stories of Mark are all about the disciples, not about Jesus—and there is not a single story in which a disciple looks good. They have found out who he is; now they're going to find out who they are! I think this is the typical pattern in your spiritual life and mine. We have to become Christians before we find out how deep the sin is in us. I never felt as guilty before I was converted as I have felt a million times since. A person has to be born again to get any sensitivity to his or her own sins.

So now the disciples begin to find out who they are. Jesus grimly tells them, "You don't think the way I think."

They come down from the Mount of Transfiguration and he says, "Don't tell anybody until I rise from the dead." But they don't know what he's talking about (Mark 9:9-10).

They get to the foot of the hill and meet a man whose son is possessed with a demon. The man tells Jesus, "Your disciples went through this country recently, delivering the demoniacs. I brought my son to them and now they've lost the power you had given them." (Doesn't that sound like the contemporary church?) So Jesus heals the boy and explains to the disciples, "This kind can come out only through prayer" (Mark 9:29). Again, they are mystified. Haven't they been praying hard enough?

Jesus says he is going to Jerusalem to be arrested and executed, then to rise from the dead. Once more, Mark notes, "They did not understand what he was saying and were afraid to ask him" (Mark 9:32).

They get to the end of the day and Jesus says, "What were you arguing about on the way?" (v. 33). They blush with shame because they were arguing over who was going to be first in the Kingdom. Jesus sighs wearily. In essence, he says, "You still don't understand. My Kingdom is not ordered in that way. Unless you become as a little child, you can't be a part of my Kingdom" (see vv. 34-37).

John says, "Well, Lord, we did one good thing today."

"What was that?" Jesus asks.

"We found a fellow casting out devils in your name and we forbade him, because he's not one of us." Imagine! The disciples could not help the man who had the demoniac son; but now they're rebuking someone who has the power they once had, but have lost!

The rest of the Gospel of Mark is a succession of stories about the disciples' failure to understand what Jesus is trying to accomplish. The stories prove repeatedly that Jesus' closest followers did not think as he thought. Is all of that accidental? I think not. The first step in the Christian life is to find out who Christ is. The second step, after you become a Christian, is to find out who you are. Everything negative about Jesus' disciples recorded in Mark 8:27–16:20 is turned around in the first six chapters of Acts. So far as I can see, they did not have "the mind of Christ" until Pentecost.

"The Carnal Mind" vs. "The Mind of Christ"

While the Bible says that few people have possessed the "mind of Christ," it also emphasizes that God calls his people to this place of intimate communion with him. This is not an experience reserved for some kind of spiritual elite corps. Unless we Christians have "the mind of Christ," we will be handicapped in our efforts to serve the Lord.

Sadly, this spiritual handicap has plagued the church from the very beginning. Paul warned the Christians at Rome and Corinth that many of them were "carnally minded," rather than having the "mind of Christ" (see Rom. 8:6-8; 1 Cor. 3:1). They were locked in continual power struggles within the church. They lusted after the same things that unconverted people want. They could not grasp even the most elementary teachings of spiritual things, because they remained spiritually immature. They were the most weak and ineffectual citizens of the Kingdom of God.

I am convinced that every great revival in the history of the church has started when God's people began to seek "the mind of Christ." When they set aside the normal human way of thinking about the world and allowed Christ to direct their lives, the world has been turned "upside down" (Acts 17:6).

In the course of this study, I want to share with you the true stories of several people who've had such an experience. Let me begin with a man I met about four years ago. When he was 26, this fellow was challenged by a missionary to live for Christ. So he said, "I decided to see if a man could live for Christ in Ford Motor Company." God blessed him and he advanced through the ranks of the company. Eventually, he was moved up to a more strategic and more powerful position as vice-president.

One day, after a particularly rough siege at the office, he came home and said to his wife, "Phyllis, I need a few minutes alone. I need some time to pray. Can you hold supper?" She said, "Yes." So he went into his study and shut the door. There he stretched out flat on the carpet and said, "Lord, nothing's going right."

The Lord said, "That's right."

He said, "Lord, there's something really wrong."

The Lord said, "That's right."

He said, "Lord, what is it?"

The Lord said, "You're in the wrong place."

"Lord, what do you mean, I'm in the wrong place?"

"I don't want you working for Ford Motor Company anymore."

"Lord, did you know that Ford is looking for a new president and I am on the 'short list'?"

And the Lord said, "Yes, I know that."

"Did you know that my buddies tell me I'm on the top of the 'short list'?"

"Yes, I know about that."

"Lord, do you know what it would cost me if I left Ford Motor Company now? It would cost me 10 to 20 million dollars!"

"So what?"

"Well, Lord, what do you want me doing if you don't want me working for Ford Motor Company?"

The Lord said, "Joe, you have a great gift for interpersonal relationships. I want you in hospice work, helping people die."

So Joe Kordick resigned as a vice-president of Ford Motor Company and began working with people who were dying.

One day, the hospice people said to him, "We have an AIDS case. Would you take him? Nobody else on our staff is willing to help him." His first shift with the AIDS patient was to be from 7:00 in the evening until 12:00 midnight. Such a long stint is unusual in hospice work, but it had been so long since the family had any relief, and they wanted to visit some of their relatives.

Before that night, the hospice staff told Joe that he must never touch the man; he must wear special clothes and rubber gloves. But when Joe got ready to go in, he thought, *Wait a minute. This man is a fellow human being for whom Christ died. I'm not going to wear all of that special uniform and rubber gloves.* So he walked into the bedroom of the AIDS patient without them. He went over to the bed, leaned down, put his arms around the pitiful man, and hugged him to himself.

The AIDS patient looked up hostilely and said, "Who are you? Why are you here?"

Joe said, "My name's Joe Kordick and I'm here because I love you. One day Jesus Christ came into my heart and put his love inside me, so I love you."

"Oh," the AIDS patient said, "so you're one of those religious birds, are you?"

"You got it exactly right," Joe said. "I'm one of those guys."

"Well, at least you touched me," the patient said. "Nobody else has."

That evening, Joe learned the AIDS patient's story. He was not related in any way to the family with whom he was living. He had been the homosexual lover of their son. He had contracted AIDS first and it was he who gave AIDS to their son. When the family found that their son had AIDS, they asked him to come home. Their son had said, "I won't come unless I can bring my lover." They thought, *Well, the lover got AIDS first so he'll die first. Then we'll have our son for awhile to ourselves.* So the two young men moved into the family's apartment. The family was so humiliated, they never told anybody in the apartment building that they had two AIDS patients there. Soon after the two homosexuals moved in, the family's son died. They were left taking care of the man they felt had murdered their son. You can imagine the hostility in that apartment. That was what Joe walked into.

Joe paused, then looked at me and said, "Dennis, he died a short time later. But I won him to Jesus. I know I'm going to meet him in heaven."

Do you know what I think is the key to that whole story? Joe Kordick came to the place, through the grace of God, where he cared more about the AIDS patient than he cared about himself. That AIDS patient then had the chance of redemption. That's not our normal way of thinking about things, but it's the way Christ thinks. Christ came to deliver us from the destructive tyranny of self-interest.

Questions We Need to Ask

You may ask, "How can I get to that kind of place?" I believe that's a vitally important question, and I believe the answer must come from the Word of God. I have written this book to delve into what the Bible says about having "the mind of Christ."

What does the Bible mean when it says we can have "the mind of Christ"? Is this a normative experience for every Christian, or can we expect only a few to undergo this change? How *do* we get to the kind of place where we think as Christ thinks? Does it occur at the time of conversion, before conversion, or after?

Most pointedly, what changes can you expect when you have the mind of Christ? How will the church be different—indeed, how will the world be different—if you "let the same mind be in you that was in Christ Jesus" (Phil. 2:5)?

These are the questions I want to address in the following chapters.

2

Doing Right or Being Righteous?

The essence of sin is self-interest. Sin shows itself among un-regenerate people in the more "fleshly" sins and the flagrant mani-festations of autonomy, as individuals seek to determine their own destiny. But the regenerated person is not necessarily cleansed from that self-interest. While regeneration breaks the tyranny of self-interest, the deliverance is not yet complete. To the extent that self-interest still influences us, every aspect of our lives will be set at cross purposes with God.

Most theologians approach the subject of sin from an entirely different direction. They begin with the proposition that sin is the transgression of God's law. This results in an inadequate assessment of the moral problem of humanity, since it distorts the character of the relationship between God and us.

I can best illustrate this with a remarkable story found in Genesis 16. It is the story of Abram, Hagar, and Ishmael. For a long time, I was sorry that God left this story in the Bible, because it is a blot on the testimony of our spiritual father, Abram. I have come to understand, however, that it illustrates how a devout, law-abiding person may still be sinning against God. For this reason, I believe this story sheds helpful light on the true nature of sin.

As this chapter begins, Abram is 85 years of age and Sarai is 75. Ten years have passed since God said to Abram, "I will make of you a great nation, and I will bless you, and make your name great, so that you will be a blessing…. And in you all the families of the earth shall be blessed" (Gen. 12:2-3). Ten long years have passed and God has not kept his promise. Now Sarai comes to Abram and says, "We need to do something. You've told everybody in this country that God is going to give us a son. You've put God in an awful spot. Don't you think we ought to help him out?" (Always beware when someone wants to help God out!)

"By the way, Abram," Sarai may have said, "when God told you that he was going to give you a son, did he ever mention me?" If you will carefully read the Scripture, you will find that God did not mention Sarai in any of those conversations with Abram until after Ishmael was born. So she says, "You see that the Lord has prevented me from bearing children; go in to my slave-girl; it may be that I shall obtain children by her" (Gen. 2).

This suggestion seems very peculiar to our modern ears. But we need to understand the culture in which it was said.

When I was in graduate school, I had the privilege of reading the Code of Hammurabi very carefully; it was the prevailing law code in the ancient world of the Near East. That law code tells a woman who can't have a son exactly what she ought to do. In the ancient world, the main purpose of marriage was to provide a man with an heir to receive the family's possessions and name. So if a married woman could not fulfil her function, the Code of Hammurabi gave her some options. She could take one of her servant girls, give that girl to her husband, and let her husband have a son through the servant girl. The law code clearly states that when the son is born, the son does not belong to the mother. Instead, the son legally belongs to the wife who gave the servant to the father. Everything that Sarai and Abram did in this story was in strict accordance with the laws of their time.

So Abram slept with Hagar and she conceived a son. Eventually, Hagar seemed to act a bit uppity toward her mistress, who was still barren. Sarai dealt harshly with her, so the servant girl took her son Ishmael and fled to the desert. Again, all of this was done in accordance with the Code of Hammurabi. Another fifteen years later, long after this tragic detour from God's plan, Sarai conceived and bore Isaac to Abram in his old age.

Our Problem and Our Potential

The story of Abram and Sarai underscores why our modern evangelical views of sin and redemption are sorely inadequate to explain the full scope of our problem, or God's response to that problem. Contrary to the currently popular view, Christ did not come into this world to restore our obedience to God's law. Obedience was involved in his mission; but obedience was not the essence of his divine sonship. Nor is obedience the essence of divine spousehood, which corresponds to our relationship with the heavenly Father, as the Bride of Christ.

Love is more than obedience, just as estrangement is more than disobedience.

Abram and Sarai were fully obedient to man's law and fully obedient to God's law, so far as they understood it. Yet they interfered with God's will for their lives, because they did not believe God would miraculously accomplish what he had promised them. In their eager desire to find an heir, they engineered their own way to do what God had already assured them he would do.

What then is God's intention for our lives? Does God simply expect us to live in conformity to his law? If we believe that, then we misunderstand the full extent of our human fallenness. We misunderstand as well the nature of the redemption Christ brings.

Many of my Reformed colleagues believe that God is a Sovereign who orders the affairs of our world by unilateral, irresistible decree. However, I believe this concept leads to a defective view of God, of man, of sin, and of salvation. I am convinced that sovereignty is a secondary category applied to God. Sovereignty could not have been a part of God's experience until the Creation, when he had subjects to rule.

The primary category for God was established by the relationships within his triune personhood, where his fatherhood existed prior to his sovereignty. First Corinthians 15:24-28 says that Christ will deliver his kingdom back to his Father, from whence it came. Note that God is described in this consummately eschatological passage as Father, not as King. Also note that Romans 8:29 describes Christ as the "firstborn among a large family," not the first in a retinue of servants.

While the categories of God's sovereignty and our servanthood are biblical, I think the Bible shows that they are not the primary categories for describing our relationship with God. Temporal logic shows they are not. God is eternally the Father and eternally the Son. The Father-Son relationship existed within the Trinity long before there were subjects for the King. In the bosom of eternity, one Person of the Trinity was able to address another as "Father," but none addressed another as "Lord."

God created us through the Son and for the Son. The intent of God's creation was to make a Bride for his Son, not subjects for him. This fact should be fundamental to our view of the Kingdom of God and our potential as citizens of the Kingdom.

You see, if God's purpose in the Creation was to make subjects for Christ, then the purpose of the Kingdom of God would be to subdue all Creation to him—to assert the supreme ascendancy of his power. Yet the Bible does not portray God or man in this context. In fact, Genesis 1–2 portrays man as the master of creation. The Bible says God granted man the responsibility of exercising dominion over what God had created. A king does not give his subjects such prerogatives—but a king gives those prerogatives to his children!

The crux of our sin problem is also the center of our soul's potential. The essence of sin is self-interest and our sinful state is estrangement from God. By contrast, God wants us to live in full communion with him. When we do, we will no longer be dominated by self-interest.

Instead of devising our own way through life, we will seek God's way. Instead of applying our energies to fulfil our desires, we will seek to fulfil his desires. Instead of being self-serving, we will be self-sacrificing.

Abram Was Right, But…

Abram was deeply religious. He is the first person with whom the Bible connects the word *believe*. Notice what we read in Genesis 15: "[God] brought him outside and said, 'Look toward heaven and count the stars, if you are able to count them.' Then he said to him, 'So shall your descendants be.' And he believed the Lord, and the Lord reckoned it to him as righteousness" (vv. 5-6). The Hebrew word translated here as "believe" is also the root of our English word, *amen*. George Herbert Livingston says, "Basically, it means that Abram grounded himself in the integrity of God. In response, God accepted this act of faith as an act of righteousness which discounted the previous doubting."[1]

Abram believed that God was telling him the truth. Abram staked his future on God's promise. Abram directed his life to say, "Amen," to the will of God. And yet….

Even then, Abram did not grasp the awesome power of the God he was dealing with. Devout, religious, God-fearing Abram thought he had to devise his own way to actualize God's promises in his life. The Bible repeatedly points to Abram as the pioneer of our faith (Rom. 4:1-5; Gal. 3:6-9; Heb. 11:8-12). I have no question that Abram received from God the gift of eternal life. I think it is equally clear that Abram did not think as God thinks, and the results have been tragic for generations that followed.

William Temple, former Archbishop of Canterbury, once said that if your concept of God is wrong, the more religion you get, the more dangerous you become to yourself and everyone else. That statement certainly applies to Abram.

Think of the centuries-old conflict that has developed between the descendants of Isaac (the Jews) and the descendants of Ishmael (the Muslims). The hottest powder keg in the world today is the result of Abram's liaison with Hagar. The American Secretary of State goes repeatedly to Palestine to try to contain the conflict between the children of Hagar and the children of Sarah.

Something is inexorably destructive when we try to act according to mere human reasoning. When we insert our way into the will of God, tragedy ultimately comes. So the Holy Spirit very lovingly rebukes us, chastens us, and draws us back, so that we live in the Spirit and not according to our own way.

I had just finished a board meeting in Chicago and was standing in O'Hare Airport, waiting for my flight. Another member of the same board was standing with me. He is a man with whom I have developed quite an intimate friendship. Our gates were near each other, so we continued to talk as we waited for our planes. He said, "Dennis, I'd like to tell you a personal story. I found Christ as a young person. God called me to preach in my teens. I went to the university, finished my training, then graduated from seminary. I took a pastorate and began my pastoral ministry. God was good and blessed my ministry, and my church began to grow. I moved on to a larger church and it began to grow. But as I preached and worked in the church, I began to find an emptiness in my heart. One day, I came into my study, locked the door behind me, and laid down on my face on the floor. I began to say, 'Lord, if this is all there is, I don't know if it's worth it or not. Isn't there something you can do for me, so that I can have the power to live the Christian life with some kind of effectiveness, joy, and meaning?'"

He said, "Dennis, it's difficult for me to tell you what happened at that point. It's as if I were a briefcase. God picked me up and turned me upside down, then he began to shake me. And as he shook, I was appalled at what began falling out of my life. Impurity, pride, arrogance, unbelief, all of the evidences of carnality within me began to fall out there. He shook me until I wondered if there would be anything left.

"Then it was as if he stopped shaking and turned me right side up. He poured himself in and filled me completely. That fiery, holy Presence just permeated every corner of my being. I don't know whether this really happened or not—I had turned the light off and in the darkness I had done my praying—yet I felt the room was filled with the light and glory of God. I decided I wouldn't tell anybody about it, but my life and my ministry were transformed.

"A few weeks after that, I was having a meeting with my pastoral staff. We finished our agenda. I noticed that nobody moved. All of my staff were looking at the same person. I thought, *Something's up!* The person they were all looking at said very hesitantly, "Pastor, we have a question we would like to ask you."

"I said, 'Go ahead.'

"So the person speaking said, 'We've been watching you and we think something's happened to you. If it has, would you tell us what it was?'

"So I told them what had happened to me. Then I said, 'Don't tell anybody.'

"A few weeks after that, I was in a board meeting. We finished our business and nobody moved. I noticed everybody was looking at the chairman, so I knew something was up. The chairman started very hesitantly and said, 'Pastor, we have a very personal question we'd like to ask you. You may not want to answer it.'

"I said, 'Well, try me.'

"The chairman of the board said, 'We've been talking. We think something's happened to you. And if it has, whatever it is, we like it. We'd like you to tell us about it.'

"So I told them about how God had come in his Holy Spirit to fill and cleanse my heart. They said, 'Well, we like the change, Pastor.'"

My friend paused and the noise of O'Hare Airport seemed to fade in the background. Then he said, "You know, Dennis, they didn't like it nearly as much as I did! Because now the discord within my heart was gone. The presence of Christ was richer than it had ever been before."

His experience proves, as Abram's experience proves, that a devout person may still be far from the heart of God. Job is another example. "That man was blameless and upright," the Bible says, "one who feared God and turned away from evil" (Job 1:1). Then hardship and suffering fell upon Job. Disaster stripped away all of his possessions, his children, and even his health. In the depths of despair, Job cried that it would have been better if he had not been born. Surely, God made an error by bringing him into this world. God patiently heard Job's bitter complaints. Then he asked, "Who is this that darkens counsel by words without knowledge?... Will you even put me in the wrong? Will you condemn me that you may be justified?" (Job 38:2; 40:8). Job's heart was stung by those questions. He repented of his resentful thoughts toward God. In the end, he realized that every blessing was a gift from God, not a reward for his own goodness.

Not Enough To Believe What's Right

Abram's experience proves that we need more than correct belief to live in harmony with God. Abram's faith opened the door for God's blessing. Abram's confidence in God allowed God to redeem him. So Abram's beliefs, true as they were, could not accomplish what God in his gracious love did for him.

Here is another trap into which we modern evangelicals have fallen. We have drifted into the notion that right thinking makes right living. So we have become obsessed with testing the orthodoxy of one another's beliefs. Yet the hotter the doctrinal debates become, the colder the hearts of those who wrangle about doctrines.

Hear me. I believe that right thinking and orthodox doctrine are vitally important to the life of the church. However, right thinking is not enough.

Had Abram been the world's most sophisticated theologian, all of his beliefs could not have saved him from the penalty of sin. Had he been the most astute philosopher who ever lived, Abram could not have reasoned his way into thinking as God thinks. Only a personal encounter with God himself could bring that change to Abram's life, or to yours and mine.

The current vogue is to seek God by introspection or philosophical speculation. Both are expressions of self-interest, so such efforts are doomed to fail, because God seldom blesses our self-serving intents. At the same time, God knows the true desires of the heart, and he is a rewarder of those who diligently seek him. So even the person who begins this quest in a self-serving way can sometimes be caught unaware by God.

That was the experience of the Frenchman Blaise Pascal, who sought the ultimate truth of life through mathematics, physics, and philosophy. Pascal proved himself to be a genius in each of those fields, yet he had not found what he was seeking.

He tried religious meditation under a spiritual director. He studied the Scriptures. He spent watchful nights in fasting and prayer. This too seemed to be a dead end...until God found him! Pascal scribbled his thoughts that night on a slip of paper, which he stitched into the lining of his coat and carried with him to his dying day. That slip of paper is now preserved in the National Library of Paris. Translated, Pascal's note says:

> Year of Grace 1654
>> Monday 23 November, feast of St. Clement,...
>
> From about half past ten at night to about half an hour after midnight,
>> FIRE
>
> "God of Abraham, God of Isaac, God of Jacob" (Exodus 3:6),
>> not of philosophers and scholars.
>
> Certitude, heartfelt joy, peace.
> God of Jesus Christ....
> "My God and Your God" (John 20:17).
> "Your God shall be my God" (Ruth 1:16).
> The world forgotten, everything except God....
> "O righteous Father, the world has not known You, but I have
>> known You" (John 17:25).
>
> Joy, Joy, Joy, tears of joy....
> May I never be separated from him.[2]

We must come to know God on his own terms. If we seek him merely to satisfy our intellectual vanity, we will be disappointed. But if we earnestly want to know and serve him, we shall find him—or, more likely, he will find us!

Not Enough to Desire What's Right

The Old Testament teaches that we are incapable of serving God faithfully until our minds are transformed to be like his. God says through the prophet Isaiah:

> For my thoughts are not your thoughts,
> nor are my ways your ways, says the Lord.
> For as the heavens are higher than the earth,
> so are my ways higher than your ways
> and my thoughts than your thoughts (Isa. 55:8-9).

But this is not to be our permanent fate. Scripture holds forth the thrilling promise that we can have his Spirit within us, so that we desire what God desires and strive for the things that he would achieve. He says through Ezekiel, "A new heart I will give you, and a new spirit I will put within you; and I will remove from your body the heart of stone and give you a heart of flesh. I will put my spirit within you, and make you follow my statutes and be careful to observe my ordinances" (Ezek. 36:26-27).

Why would God challenge the people of Israel with the fact that his mind was set on different priorities, unless it was possible for them to think as he does? Why would God promise to put a new spirit within them, unless he planned to do that very thing?

Hannah Whitall Smith said, "Our will is a piece of splendid machinery, a sort of governor, such as in a steam engine to regulate the working of the steam; everything depends on the intelligence that guides its action—our ignorance or God's wisdom. As long as our own ignorance is the guide, the whole machinery is sure to go wrong, and it is dangerous for us to say 'I will' or 'I will not.' But when we have surrendered the working of our wills to God, we are letting him work in us 'to will and to do of his good pleasure' (Phil. 2:13)."[3]

Not Enough to Do What's Right

Reuben Welch, who grew up in the Church of the Nazarene, said that his mother's teaching on ethical living could be summed up in just two words: "Do right." Sadly, that often has been the sum and substance of what we have tried to teach the next generation. I suppose it comes out of the emphasis that our spiritual forebears in the nineteenth-century holiness revival placed on right conduct. They were admonished not to smoke, not to dance, not to wear revealing clothes, and so on. They learned that, above all else, they must strive to "do right."

Abram reveals the flaw in such thinking. Abram did what was right in terms of Hammurabi's law. He did what was right in terms of striving to fulfil God's plan. But he was tragically wrong because he acted outside of God's leading.

Dare I say it? We have too many Christian people who "do right" with the wrong motives. They "do right" to advance themselves or to obtain some recognition for themselves or to receive some kind of reward for themselves. That's self-interest. We said at the outset of this chapter that self-interest is the essence of sin. Why? Because self-interest is diametrically opposed to the character of God.

God calls us beyond merely "doing right." He calls us to be people who live in his way because we have his own heart (Jer. 32:39). He calls us to be changed into his righteous people by the transforming power of his Holy Spirit. Right living results from the transformation of a person's mind and heart, rather than from any kind of self-imposed discipline.

Our Way vs. God's Way

I am impressed by something else about Abram. Notice that Abram got through Hagar everything that he got through Sarai—except the most important thing.

God had promised Abram a son out of whom would come a family, out of whom would come a nation, and to whom he would give real estate. Isaac had twelve sons; Ishmael also had twelve sons. Isaac's twelve sons had families, became kings with kingdoms, and they owned great sections of the Middle East; the same was true of Ishmael's sons. So Abram got everything through Hagar that he got through Sarai—except his long-awaited descendant, Jesus. Ishmael was the child of Abram's perfect conformity to the law, while Isaac was the child of God's perfect fulfillment of his promise. A simple biological act could produce Ishmael, but it took an act of God to produce Isaac.

Where God does not act, nothing is ultimately redemptive. All salvation is in God; it is not in us. The best that you and I can do is still "carnal," if that's all it is. It is very easy for us to do our best and assume that's what God wants. After all, that's what Abram did. But nothing eternal takes place until God acts.

The Bible holds before us the promise that we can live in full communion with God here and now. We can have his heart, his outlook, his priorities, his goals and objectives here and now. The Bible extends to us an invitation to begin walking with God now. We need not wait to receive some new mystical insight in order for this promise to be fulfilled. It is a present reality for those who have the Spirit and heart of God, as he promised to give us.

That is God's vision for us: "The nations shall know that I am the Lord, says the Lord God, when through you I display my holiness before their eyes" (Ezek. 36:23).

Sacrifice and Sanctification

God called Abraham to leave his country, his kindred, and his household—the things that gave him security, identity, and fulfillment. He called Abraham to leave a place of cultural refinement and go to the hinterlands of the Palestinian hills, though all the traffic was going the other way! Why? Because he wanted Abraham to be his priest, the middleman between God and all the nations of the earth (Gen. 18:22-23). God called him to sacrifice the things he held most precious, so that he would dedicate himself to the Lord alone. Nowhere is this made more clear than in Abraham's sacrifice of his son, Isaac.

In 1979, I read the Gospels in a modern Israeli Hebrew translation. The same day I was reading John 3 in this Israeli version, I was translating Genesis 22, which recounts the sacrifice of Isaac. Three times in that narrative, God tells Abraham to sacrifice "your son, your only son" (Heb., *ben-yom, ben-yaqi*). This Old Testament Hebrew idiom emphasizes the preciousness of one's only child. Oddly enough, I found the same phrase in the modern Israeli version of John 3:16, "For God so loved the world that he gave his *ben*, his *ben-yaqi*, that whosoever believes in him should not perish but have everlasting life."

The coincidence of these two readings struck me. I could imagine myself standing on Mount Moriah as Abraham raised the knife to kill Isaac, when God's angel stopped him, saying, "Abraham, do not touch the lad." I heard the second Person of the Trinity say to the first Person, "Father, we are coming back here someday, aren't we?"

And the Father said, "Yes, in about nineteen hundred years."

"The next time it won't be one of them on the altar, will it?" I heard the Son ask.

"No," the Father said. "The next time you will be there."

"Father, when the Roman soldiers are about to put the spikes through my hands and feet, will you say, 'Do not touch the lad'?"

And I thought I heard the Father say, "No, Son. We never ask them to do in symbol what we have not done in reality."

Abraham sacrificed everything he had to become the intermediary between God and the nations. This is why Abraham is our model of faith.[4]

Jesus is the ultimate illustration of what God called Abraham to do: Jesus emptied himself of position, possessions, and all that he had, in order to be our Priest.

If God called Abraham to do what he called his Son to do, does he not call us to do the same?

Abraham's descendants, the nation of Israel, became God's priests to the world (Exod. 19:6; Isa. 61:6). The people of the church are called to be his priests to the world today (1 Pet. 2:5; Rev. 1:6). This means we do not live for our own sakes. The central motive of our call is to be other-oriented. How can we do this unless we are freed from self-interest?

In order to be God's priests today, we must have an Abrahamic detachment from the earthly things that would otherwise give us identity, security, and fulfillment. We must lose ourselves in order to serve God. Only by doing that can we be redemptive.

Endnotes

[1]George Herbert Livingston, *Beacon Bible Commentary: 1, Genesis* (Kansas City: Beacon Hill Press, 1969), p. 75.

[2]James M. Houston, ed., *Mind on Fire: A Faith for the Skeptical and Indifferent* (Minneapolis: Bethany House), pp. 41-42.

[3]Hannah Whitall Smith, *God Is Enough*, ed. by Melvin E. Dieter and Hallie A. Dieter (Grand Rapids: Francis Asbury Press, 1986), p. 51.

[4]Our English word *sacrifice* comes from the Latin phrase meaning "to make holy" *(sacra faciere)*. So self-sacrifice is intrinsically a part of sanctification. Indeed, sanctification is liberation from the supreme tyranny, the tyranny of self; and this is what God would accomplish in your life. Only he can do it.

3

Understanding
Who Christ Is

The Gospel of John shows that Israel did not think the way God thought. The Jews had narrowed their understanding of God's redemptive plan until the typical religious person of Jesus' day supposed that salvation was a means of taking care of oneself, excluding any consideration of God's redemptive purpose for the rest of the world.

The nation of Israel did not understand how much God cared for the entire world. For that reason, Jews could not believe how far God was willing to go in order to save it. They could not believe he cared about the rest of the world as much as he did, so they could not believe Jesus was their Savior when he went to the cross.

Two of our children have served in Europe as missionaries. When our first daughter and her husband began attending language school in Paris, they needed to find someone who could babysit with their little girl. They mentioned their need to a Salvation Army captain in charge of a hostel that housed seven hundred single girls, and he sent to them a converted Jewish woman. They were surprised that the captain sent her, because she was badly crippled. She had suffered polio when she was nineteen months old, and had never taken a step without pain.

One day she asked my daughter, "Sally, is there really a God? And if there is, does he care about people like me? And if he does care, why does he let these things happen to me?"

How does one answer such questions? After a long moment of silence, Sally said, "Marie, I don't have any easy answers to all of that. But I want to tell you there is a God. He is your heavenly Father. He cares about you as any loving father would care for his child. And I believe that, when you hurt, he hurts more than you do."

One night soon afterward, Marie phoned and asked if she could come to Sally's house to talk. When they sat down together, she said, "A group of us went to a cafe this evening. We were just a bunch of single girls, laughing and enjoying ourselves. Then a French gentleman stopped at our table. He said, 'You young ladies are having a good time, aren't you? Well, this whole picture is obscene to me. I have a five-year-old daughter at home, dying of an incurable disease.'

"One of the girls in the group said, 'Sir, if your daughter is dying, you ought to pray. Maybe God will heal her!'

"He looked down at her and said bitterly, 'I've prayed more than any mortal you have ever seen. And if there is a God, he hasn't heard. Or he doesn't care.'"

Marie Cecille said, "Things got very still. I knew that one of us had to say something. So I said, 'Sir, when you stand over the bed of your five-year-old, who hurts more—you or she?'

"He responded instantly, 'I do! She's too young and naive to understand the tragedy of her situation. I hurt far more than she does.'

"'Yes,' I said, 'and while you stand over your daughter, hurting, there is a heavenly Father watching over you who hurts more than you hurt.'"

Marie told my daughter, "Sally, the moment I said that, it seemed as though God touched me and took away some of my own scar tissue!"

Jesus came to show us the Father's heart. He came to demonstrate that "God so loved the world that he gave his only Son" to die for us (John 3:16). Because the first-century Jews did not understand that, they did not recognize Christ for who he was.

Symbols of the King

We wonder how the Jews and their religious leaders missed Jesus. The reasons they gave for rejecting him were the very reasons they should have accepted him. That was one of the marks of their sinful self-centeredness: They saw things backwards. We often miss him for the same reason.

God loved us so much that he came and lived among us. He stooped to become a mortal man. As one of Charles Wesley's hymns says:

> Our God, ever blest, with oxen doth rest;
> Is nursed by his creature, and hangs at the breast.

How far God was willing to go in order to reach you and me! We don't expect to find God among the oxen, but that's where Jesus was. We don't expect the sovereign God to enter this world in the form of a baby, but that's how he came. And we don't expect the One on whom our existence depends to be dependent on one of us, but he was. God loved us so much that he was willing to reverse our roles. He became one of us so that we might have his nature and have fellowship with him. What an awesome truth! Because it is so awesome, the Jews missed him—and so do many of us.

The Jews knew that the Christ would come as a king. A king enters his kingdom with a throne, a crown, a scepter, and a retinue of servants ready to do his bidding—the symbols of his power. Yet, when Jesus the King of kings entered his kingdom, that is not the way he came. Four symbols in the Gospel of John depict the regal power of Jesus; but those symbols contradicted the world's understanding of a king.

The Rejectable King

The first symbol is suggested by the prologue to John's Gospel, where we are told that Jesus "came to his own home, and his own people received him not" (1:11, RSV). John expands upon this image in the Book of Revelation, as Jesus says, "Listen! I am standing at the door, knocking; if you hear my voice and open the door, I will come in to you and eat with you, and you with me" (Rev. 3:20).

I have been deeply impressed by Holman Hunt's painting entitled *The Light of the World*, which hangs at St. Peter's Cathedral in London. It depicts Jesus standing at a door and knocking. Hunt shows Jesus wearing a king's robe and a priest's garment; so he is the Intercessor-King. He wears a crown upon his head and carries a lantern in his hand; hence, the title, *The Light of the World*. But Jesus knocks at a door that has no handle, no way of opening it from his side. Greenery has grown over the door frame, suggesting it has been a very long time since that door was opened, if it ever was.

I first saw that painting when I visited London in 1955; I saw it again in 1974. When I viewed it a second time, I thought, *Nineteen years have passed, and he is still knocking.* No head of state has to knock at anyone's door. The President of the United States does not knock at doors; someone goes before him to open them! His aides are sure that the President never gets in a situation where he can be rejected, for that would be a snub to the nation he represents. No President can afford a public image of rejection.

Yet the King of kings came into the world as One who knocks—One who is vulnerable and rejectable. The Jews did not expect that. They wanted a king who would come in power and pomp to expel the Romans from their land. Yet Jesus came, not to deal with the Roman menace, but to see whether his people would accept him. So he knocked and he knocked…and he is knocking still.

The Humble King

The second image of the Messiah appears three and a half years later in John's narrative, as Jesus enters the city of Jerusalem on Palm Sunday. The people of the city have heard about his miracles; they know about his power. Just a few days before, not far from the city, Jesus raised Lazarus from the dead (11:1-44). Spectators to that event have spread the word throughout the capital city. By Palm Sunday, everyone in Jerusalem has talked with Lazarus, or talked with someone who had talked with Lazarus, or talked with someone who'd talked with someone who'd seen Lazarus raised from the dead! So the whole city turns out to greet Jesus. They hail him as their Messianic King. As Jesus crests the Mount of Olives and begins his descent into the city, people strip branches from the olive trees and pull the cloaks from their backs, laying them on the ground to make a pathway for him. They cry out, "Hosanna! Blessed is he who comes in the name of the Lord, even the king of Israel!" They are ready to crown him as their king.

At that moment, Jesus mounts a donkey to ride into the city. Some Bible commentators speculate that this is a kingly gesture; they theorize that royal donkeys were ridden by certain leaders of the ancient East. But I assure you that no Roman general ever entered Jerusalem on a donkey, and no Egyptian pharaoh ever had a donkey pull him in his gold-plated chariot. In the ancient world, the horse symbolized power, while the donkey was a humble beast of burden. Without question, this is a Messianic gesture. Zechariah 9:9 had predicted, "Lo, your king comes to you; triumphant and victorious is he, humble and riding on a donkey...." If we read the rest of Zechariah's prophecy, we get confirmation of the fact that Jesus' riding on the donkey is an intentional act of Messianic fulfillment: "He will cut off the chariot...and the war-horse from Jerusalem" (Zech. 9:10). It is as if Jesus were telling the exultant crowd, "I am not the kind of king you expect. I am not coming in physical power or military might. I come, not to impose something upon you, but to offer you redemption. So I come meekly."

Most of us like the "horse" style of dealing with other people, rather than the "donkey" style. The horse is a symbol of worldly glory; we like to have the admiration that a horse rider can command. But Jesus does not come to seek glory; he comes to serve, not to be served. So he rides on a donkey. The Jews, who had great ambitions for their Messiah, could not understand why he did this.

The Servant King

The third kingly symbol is seen the following Thursday night, as Jesus takes his disciples to an upper room to observe the Passover meal. There he takes a basin and towel, kneels on the floor, and begins washing their feet. Peter looks incredulously at him and says, "Lord, are you going to wash my feet?" Jesus says, "You do not know now what I am doing, but later you will understand" (13:7).

Imagine the trauma in Peter's heart that night. Finally, he says, "Lord, not my feet only but also my hands and my head!" (13:9). Jesus says that is not necessary. He simply wants Peter and all of his disciples to know that he is their servant.

If you are offended by the idea of Jesus being your servant, you have the same problem Peter had. You still think as the world thinks, not as God thinks.

The Self-Sacrificing King

The fourth unexpected symbol of the Messiah is found in John's narrative of Good Friday. Dorothy Sayers said that human history is replete with examples of men and women dying for their gods, but who could have imagined a God who would die for his people? So it was on Good Friday.

As the people of Jerusalem viewed the cross, they must have thought, *There is conclusive proof that this fellow is not the Christ: he dies like any other man. He is an imposter!* They rejected him for exactly the reason that they should have fallen at his feet and adored him, because their salvation came through Jesus' sacrifice of himself.

The Jews' reasons for rejecting Jesus were half right. Normally, kings do come with thrones, crowns, and retinues. When Jesus returns, he will come with all those symbols of power. Read the Book of Revelation with that in mind, and you will notice that Jesus does not come patiently knocking on doors; he comes as a clap of lightning that bolts from the East to the West in an instant, and no door can keep him out. Every eye will behold him and every knee will bow before him. No one can shut Jesus out when he comes a second time.

When Jesus returns, he will come not on a donkey, but on a great white horse. There will be a stack of crowns on his head—bejeweled crowns of gold, not of thorns. Out of his mouth will come a sharp, flaming, two-edged sword; and across his thigh will be written the words, "King of kings and Lord of lords" (Rev. 19:11-16).

When Jesus returns, he will come not to kneel at our feet. Revelation 6 says that all the mighty leaders of earth, as well as the poor and humble, will prostrate themselves at his feet. He will not be on a cross, but on a royal throne. We disposed of him the first time he came; but when he returns, he will dispose of us.

The Book of Revelation tells us that Jesus' return will not be a new opportunity for redemption. It says he comes in power and glory, fixing everyone's destiny forever: "Let the evildoer still do evil, and the filthy still be filthy, and the righteous still do right, and the holy still be holy" (Rev. 22:11). No sins will be forgiven when Christ comes the second time; no lust will be removed from the human heart; no broken relationships will be restored. He will come again to fix us eternally as we are.

Sacrifice and Redemption

We rejected Jesus when he came in the only form that would allow him to save us. John 12 tells us that, after Jesus' triumphal entry into Jerusalem, he told his disciples, "The hour has come for the Son of Man to be glorified" (v. 23). He was referring to the cross; he knew the only way for him to accomplish his mission was to go to the cross. So he said, "Unless a grain of wheat falls into the earth and dies, it remains just a single grain; but if it dies, it bears much fruit" (v. 24).

Do you notice what the Son of God is saying? God himself cannot act redemptively without going the way of self-sacrifice.

If we wish to bear fruit for God, we must be willing to do the same. We must come to the end of ourselves; we must follow his path of vulnerability, where our lives are exposed to rejection and pain. That is the only way our lives can be redemptive. If we want our lives to be wholly his, we cannot be characterized by the pomp and circumstance of the world, any more than he was. We must be servants. Our lives must be poured out for others.

Recently, I visited a mission station and talked with a veteran missionary who had graduated from Cambridge University. He had served at the mission so effectively that the mission officials asked him to become president of their seminary. He responded, "Oh, no. That's no place for a gringo. A national leader ought to fill that post."

Then they said, "Very well. Let us make you academic dean of the seminary. A man with your credentials is needed in that position."

"Oh, no," the missionary said. "We have a national leader who can serve quite capably in that position as well. I insist that you make him the academic dean."

Soon the mission leaders began considering where these staff members should live. They felt the missionary should live in the best house on the compound. "No, the president of the seminary should live there," he said.

The next-best house? "No, the academic dean should live there," he said.

So the mission officials had no choice. They put the missionary and his family in the remaining house. It had no sink in the kitchen, so the family washed their dishes in the bathroom until one of their children contracted hepatitis. The students of the seminary visited him and wept at what they saw. "Deuteronomy says that when we have a sojourner in our midst, we are responsible for his well-being," one of them said. "We must do better by you than this." So they found better housing for the missionary and his family.

Since my visit to that mission, I have heard that the national church in that area—a church once badly divided—has begun to come together. That sounds like the work of Jesus, doesn't it? When Jesus became one of us and lived like us, redemption came from it.

I cannot say whether the missionary's attitude caused the healing that is taking place on that mission; but I know that when we are willing to spend and be spent for Jesus' sake, there will be fruit from our lives.

In a pastorate that Elsie and I served some years ago, we had difficulty finding enough people to serve in places of leadership. But one talented young woman agreed to serve as the adult Sunday school teacher. As she taught, she began to hurt some people's feelings.

One day, as I was visiting in the neighborhood, she met me at her door with tears in her eyes. "What's the trouble?" I asked.

"Oh, I've just received a petition from the adults in the church. They want me to resign as teacher of the Sunday school class."

"You can't do that," I said.

"I must do that," she replied. "The thing that breaks my heart is that I just got my husband to agree to go to church with me. I hoped he would have a chance to come to know Christ. Now we cannot go back to church, because they don't want us."

"What would you do if Christ asked you to go back?"

"He wouldn't ask me to do that."

"Are you sure?" I asked.

"If I did go back, what would happen to my husband? He would mop the middle aisle of that church with the fellow whose name heads this petition."

"Well, if you must go back to church full of bitterness and resentment, you shouldn't go. But can you go back next Sunday and pray for the woman who's going to teach your class? And can you love her?"

The woman exploded in tears. When she finally regained her composure, she said, "It would take grace to do that."

"Yes, it would," I said. "Don't you think God could give you the grace to do that?"

The next Sunday, she went. She sat there in the third row of the class and prayed for the woman who took her place. She went back to that class Sunday after Sunday. Toward the end of our tenure in that parish, as Elsie and I drove into the church lot one Sunday morning, we were flagged by the man who had headed the petition drive. He said, "Dennis, have you heard what happened to Tom?"

When I saw the expression on his face, I thought something horrible must have occurred. I supposed he was dead.

"I don't understand it," the messenger continued, "but Tom got saved last night!"

"That's impossible," I said in my naive youthfulness. "There aren't any revival meetings going on."

"I know that," the man said. "But Tom says it's so."

So I went to Tom and asked him what had happened. His eyes brimmed with tears and he said, "Last night I found God."

"How?"

"Well, you know that wife of mine. You remember what they did to her in that Sunday school class. It made me so angry that I was ready to kill them all. But every night, before we went to sleep, she would kneel beside the bed and pray for them all. While she prayed, I stewed. But while she was praying last night, I rolled out onto my knees and said, 'Honey, pray for me. I'm the one who needs it.' Beside the bed with my wife, I found God last night."

It's a universal law: Keep your life for yourself, and it will be sterile. Give it up wholly to the Lord, and it will bear fruit.

Understanding Who Christ Is

Nicodemus and his Jewish brethren loathed believing that they worshiped a God who was willing to sacrifice himself. They felt it irrational that their King would humble himself to serve the lowliest people of their society. That is why most of them rejected Jesus. In this respect, first-century Judaism foreshadowed the modern American church.

We have mastered the language of the Kingdom of God, but we know little of the full power and glory of the Kingdom. Like the Jews of that age, we have developed a parochial understanding of redemption. Like them, we tend to think only of ourselves.

Most of the modern evangelical community believes the doctrine of predestination. In its simplest form, this doctrine states that God saves a few people whom he chooses to save, and the rest of the world he passes by. When the eighteenth-century evangelist William Carey declared that the church must be concerned about the lost peoples of other lands, a church official rose to his feet and cried, "Young man, when God wants to save the heathen, he won't worry you with it!" We modern Christians may not be so blatant in our pronouncements, but we are just as narrow-minded in our understanding of God's work in the world.

Some Wesleyans have erred on the other extreme from predestination. For example, the United Methodist Church (of which I am a member) espouses universalism, the idea that *everyone* will be saved. So Methodists suppose we should be concerned to feed the hungry and to endorse political reform to free the oppressed; but we need not care about the eternal destiny of their souls. This is why the number of missionaries in the United Methodist Church has plummeted for two decades. We have found our own way of limiting the scope of God's redemptive plan.

Jesus challenged such parochial thinking. He told Nicodemus that when a person is born again, he will realize that God desires to save the whole world. The new birth opens a person's eyes to the fact that God wants to save the whole world. We pervert the message of the new birth when we suppose it is simply a way to save our own skins. We must remember how Jesus summarized the gospel in John 3:16: "God so loved the *world* that he gave his only Son…" (italics added).

Think about the consequences of your own conversion. Has your relationship with Christ given you a passion for the lost world? If not, you have done the same thing with God's truth that Nicodemus did.

Christ's global way of thinking will alter more than your thinking; it will alter your behavior. For example, it will alter the way you spend your money. Several years ago, I was audited by the Internal Revenue Service. That was a religious experience for me. I sat for hours in that quiet little office while an efficient young lady looked at every check stub from the year in question. By the time our interview ended, she knew what I cared about and what I lived for. How about you? Would you be ready to spread your check stubs before an auditor in the light of John 3:16 and say, "I've read God's Word and I live by what it says"?

Christ's global perspective will alter the value systems you teach your children. For more than twenty years, I have worked with the young people at Asbury College and Seminary; during that time, I learned a great deal about their parents. I found many young people who said, "If I'm a successful doctor/lawyer/professional person, my parents will be very pleased." That comment demonstrates how far their parents were from the heart of God. Jesus' Father had only one Son, and he was not content to keep him in the privileged position of heaven. He sent his Son to earth to win lost people back to him. Why, then, do so few Christian parents aspire to have their children pour out their lives in world evangelization? I believe that if the last generation of parents who called themselves born-again Christians had possessed the heart of their heavenly Father, we would be living in a much different world today.

Unless there is a change in the thinking of the Christian parents of America, this nation will come under a judgment greater than it can imagine. Out of about forty-six thousand American missionaries now stationed in countries around the world, nearly twenty thousand will retire within the next five years, and there are few prospects for their replacement. I lay the responsibility for this impending crisis at the kitchen table, the family room, and the T.V. room of the Christian homes of this nation. The values communicated there are scarcely different from the values communicated in homes that do not pretend to love the Lord Jesus Christ.

The responsibility for world evangelization does not rest solely with the young, either. The retired people of America have more freedom to choose what they will do with their time than any other people who have ever lived. What are Christian retirees doing about prayer? How much time do they spend interceding for the world?

Few of us have exposed ourselves to the heart of God, so that we sense how deeply he cares about our lost planet. Through prayer we can begin to see the world as he sees it; we can begin to reach the world.

The Pharisees didn't accept Jesus, because they expected him to be a very different kind of King. They didn't think as God thinks. Their limited perspective blinded them to the amazing plan of God. What do you expect of him? Your expectations will shape what God is able to do for you—and what he is able to do through you.

4

Understanding
Who We Are

Because we live in a day of the précis and proposition, the Gospel of Mark is often considered to be a non-theological work. While I was studying the Gospels in college, my instructors disdained Mark as a random collection of stories, of little value for serious study. They likened it to a broken strand of pearls, which had been gathered up haphazardly so that there was no logical chronology or design to the book. They supposed that the Synoptic problem had arisen simply because the Evangelists had found different ways of restringing the episodic "pearls" from Jesus' ministry. For this reason, they felt that the Book of Romans was more useful than Mark for the study of Christian theology.

But I have become convinced that the Gospel of Mark is as carefully constructed as a Beethoven symphony. The writer had the clear intention of presenting Jesus as the Son of God, and everything he brought into the narrative had this overriding theological purpose. We seldom realize the genius of this book, however, because Mark used stories to convey his message.

I had an odd experience in this regard at Knox Presbyterian Church in Toronto, where I was speaking on the Gospel of Mark at a Wednesday evening service. At the end of the service, a very dignified looking lady approached me and said, "You cannot imagine what a relief this evening has been to me."

"What do you mean?" I asked.

"Apparently, you believe a person could be saved by reading the Gospel of Mark," she said.

"Well, I presume that's why Mark wrote the Gospel," I said, "so that people could come to a knowledge of Jesus Christ and be saved."

"What a relief!" she continued. "You see, I have a daughter who works with Wycliffe Bible Translators. She and her colleague are living among a primitive tribe. They've learned the language of those people and now are beginning to translate the Bible into that language. Of all things, they started with the Gospel of Mark. But I was sure a person couldn't be saved without understanding the Book of Romans!"

Her comment illustrates how propositionally oriented we modern evangelicals are. Further, it illustrates what a narrow understanding we have of systematic theology. We suppose that a narrative book such as Mark cannot be as theologically persuasive as Romans or some other Pauline epistle. This bias colors our personal evangelism, our preaching, and every other way we attempt to present the gospel. We assume that, if we can force someone to follow the logic of redemption, that person must be saved. That's the evangelism of power—and it's not the way most people come to a saving knowledge of Jesus Christ. Rational arguments have their place, of course; but the stories have a logical power that we dismiss too lightly.

After my conversation with the woman, I was approached by a young couple who said, "Would you like to join us for a cup of tea?"

"Oh, where is that?" I replied.

"At the Toronto Institute for Linguistics."

So I found myself sitting that evening with about ten people who had their Ph.D. degrees in linguistics, and they began discussing the message I had delivered. They began comparing Mark with Romans in very technical linguistic terms, which I could not understand, so I asked them to clarify what they meant. One man smiled and said, "Your comparison of Mark and Romans is an example of what we

call the difference between 'linear' and 'contextual' logic. Western-
ers tend to think by linear logic, while most of the world works by
contextual logic." The best example of linear logic is the philosophical syllogism:

A. All men are mortal.
B. Dennis Kinlaw is a man.
C. Therefore, Dennis Kinlaw is mortal.

The reasoning is inexorable; the conclusion is inevitable. But
the Evangelists did not express the message in these terms, nor did
most of the biblical writers.

The Gospel of Mark demonstrates the use of contextual logic. At
the same time, it challenges the thought patterns of the natural
mind. So it has double significance for our study.

Mark is writing a definitive statement of the gospel of Jesus
Christ. At the outset, he affirms that Jesus is the "Son of God"; at the
end, we see a Roman centurion looking up at the cross and saying,
"Truly this man was the Son of God!" (Mark 15:39, NASB). So the
motivating theme of the book is Jesus Christ, the Son of God. On
another level, the Gospel of Mark spells out the stages of spiritual
growth through which Jesus took his disciples. Much of the book
revolves around Jesus' ministry to the public at large; but Jesus'
ministry to his disciples figures as significantly in the narrative.

In fact, the Gospel of Mark might be divided into two sections:
(1) the narrative of chapters 1-8, which highlights Jesus' public
ministry and is concerned with Jesus' identity, and (2) the narrative
of chapters 9-16, which shows Jesus in intimate relation with his
disciples, withdrawn from the public ministry and the trauma of his
crucifixion. Let us consider each of these sections in greater detail.

Jesus' Public Ministry (chaps. 1-8)

The first half of Mark's Gospel recounts a succession of stories
and parables that portray Jesus confronting human need of almost
every possible kind. The diversity of the stories arises from the
diversity of human need. Note the progression.

John the Baptist introduces Jesus (1:4-11). Almost immediately, Jesus goes to Capernaum and enters the synagogue to teach (1:21-28). The worshipers at the synagogue are quite impressed with his teaching, because "he taught them as one having authority" (v. 22). In other words, Jesus deals with their *intellectual need;* yet Jesus' teaching is a radical departure from what they typically heard in the synagogue. It is the sort of teaching that Emile Cailliet of Princeton encountered when he first read the Bible and saw that it "discovered me to myself." Self-revelation is a natural consequence of hearing the teachings of Jesus. His word fits the reality of our lives so perfectly that we must conclude that he knows what he is talking about—he speaks with authority.

One need not be a university professor to have intellectual questions; everyone has them. Homemakers are dying with unanswered questions of "Who am I? Why am I here? And what ought I to be?" Jesus deals with those questions. Until one understands the truth, one is unable to change; so Jesus begins his evangelism with the mind—though he does not win the mind in the coercive way that we often attempt to win it.

While Jesus is preaching, a demoniac in the crowd begins to disturb the service, so Jesus rebukes the demons within him. The demons are driven out; the man is restored to his rightful mind; and the onlookers are astounded, saying, "What is this? A new teaching! With authority he commands even the unclean spirits, and they obey him" (1:27). I can well imagine Peter thinking to himself, *Look at how Jesus drove the evil out of that fellow. I wonder if he can get the evil out of me?* Every rational person wants someone to help him deal with the evil in his own heart. We want deliverance from the evil within us. And when we meet Jesus, we sense the evil within us, more than we have under any other circumstance.

So Jesus deals first with people's *intellectual needs.* Second, he deals with their *spiritual needs*—the evil within them. Third, he deals with their *physical needs.*

Peter and Andrew, natives of Capernaum, take Jesus to their home. There they find that Peter's mother-in-law is sick, so Jesus heals her (1:29-31). As the news of her healing spreads, the neighbors begin bringing their sick friends and relatives to be touched by the Master's hand (1:32-34).

Soon afterward, on the streets of Capernaum, Jesus meets a leper who kneels before him—so close that he must look up in order to see Jesus' face (1:40ff.) According to Jewish law, a leper had no right to do that. Lepers could have no contact with those who were well, for fear that the leper might defile them. Jewish law was so strict on this point that a person was considered to be unclean if he stood downwind of a leper and felt the breeze that blew across the diseased person. Then the defiled person had to be ceremonially cleansed. But Jesus permits the leper to approach him. To the surprise of the bystanders, Jesus places his hand on the head of the leper and heals him.

That episode is a dramatic demonstration of who Jesus is. It is an act far more persuasive than any propositions Jesus could have uttered about himself. It is more persuasive than all the rabbinical teaching about leprosy, which attempted to channel the Holy Spirit's healing power through superstition and ceremony.

Now Jesus disappears from Capernaum; I suspect he left the town to give people an opportunity to talk about what they had seen. No doubt they wondered, *Who is this Jesus? How does he do these things?* Chapter 2 shows Jesus returning to Capernaum. When he does, his friends do not need a telephone committee to gather a crowd; the word of his arrival spreads immediately. People probably say, "He's back!" And no one needs to ask, "Who's 'he?'" Capernaum has been buzzing with talk about Jesus, so the house is jammed with curious onlookers (2:2).

A paralytic is brought by his four friends, who lower him through the roof. Jesus tells him, "Son, your sins are forgiven" (2:5).

At that point, I imagine one Pharisee nudges another and asks, "What did he say?"

"I thought he said that fellow's sins were forgiven!"

With some apoplexy, the first growls, "That's what I thought he said! It is blasphemy! Who can forgive sins but God alone?" (2:7).

Immediately, the Pharisees get the idea that Jesus is trying to convey through these events: he is not a mere wonder worker, for the ancient world has plenty of those. While the wonders attract the people's attention and prove Jesus' compassionate response to their needs, the important thing Jesus is conveying through these events is that *he is God in the flesh.*[1]

Jesus comes into direct conflict with the Jewish Sabbath restrictions as he and his disciples pass through a field on the Sabbath and begin harvesting grain. The Pharisees ask, "Look, why are they doing what is not lawful on the sabbath?" (2:24).

Jesus says, "The sabbath was made for humankind, and not humankind for the sabbath; so the Son of man is lord even of the sabbath" (vv. 27-28).

This sets the stage for the next episode, in which Jesus heals a man with a withered hand—heals him in the synagogue on the Sabbath (3:1-6). The Pharisees challenge Jesus again. (He seems to have been under perpetual surveillance from the time he left John's crowd at the Jordan.) After the healing in the synagogue, the Pharisees begin plotting to kill Jesus.

Why do the Pharisees perceive this healing as such a subversive act? Because Jesus declares that the Sabbath had been created to honor him, not he to honor the Sabbath; immediately, the Pharisees know that Jesus is claiming to be God. That is the ultimate challenge to their authority, and it signs the death warrant for Jesus.

Other stories in Mark portray Jesus dealing with the needs of the people he met—quieting the storm at sea (chap. 4), casting out the demons named Legion (chap. 5), feeding five thousand hungry men with their women and children (chap. 6), and so on. All of these stories convey profound theology; they depict Jesus as the Sovereign Creator, who can marshal the forces of his creation to provide for the needs of his creatures.

The stories of Mark tumble over one another until they are interlocked. We see this in Jesus' encounter with Jairus, who begs

Jesus to come home with him and heal his ailing daughter (5:21ff.). Jesus agrees to go; but on his way, he stops and says, "Who touched my garments?" Here groveling at his feet is a woman who has had an issue of blood for twelve years and had spent all of her money on physicians. She does not want to touch Jesus himself because she was unclean. But she thinks, *If I touch even his garments, I shall be made well.* And Jesus says, "Daughter, your faith has made you well…" (v. 34). At that point, Jairus' servant arrives on the scene with the news that the little girl is dead. But Jesus goes on to Jairus' house and raises his daughter from the dead; the episode illustrates that he is the Lord of life (healing the woman) and of death (raising the little girl).

Again note the progression of human needs described in Mark's Gospel: intellectual needs, spiritual needs, and physical needs. We have a tendency to concentrate on the spiritual needs of other people, but Jesus is concerned with all dimensions of the human situation. We see this for example in Jesus' healing of the demoniac, who can return to his old neighborhood, his friends, and his accustomed job (5:19-20). Jesus restores him to his place in society. We need more of an emphasis on these fuller dimensions of redemption; we need to send husbands home to their wives and children. We need to devote as much attention to social healing— interrelational healing—as Jesus did.

The stories of Mark are vignettes of human need, as multitudinous in their variety as we can imagine. And as Jesus confronts these needs, we realize his adequacy for every human situation. So the first half of Mark is about the adequacy of Jesus. Mark realizes that the world is asking, "Who is Jesus?" So he replies, "Jesus did this…and this…and this. Draw your own conclusions." It is a book of inductive theology. Faith is an induction, while knowledge is a deduction. And only faith is redemptive.[2]

Either explicitly or implicitly, the stories raise the question of who Jesus is. We hear people asking explicitly, "Who is Jesus if he can teach like this? Who is he if he has power over the demonic? Who is he if he thinks he can forgive sins? Who is he if he has power over the wind and the waves?" Oddly enough, in the first half of Mark, everyone has an answer to these questions—that is, everyone except the disciples!

His friends say, "He has gone out of his mind" (3:21), and they want to take him home. The temple officials say, "He has Beelzebub" (3:22), and they want to exorcize him. The people of his hometown say, "Is not this the carpenter, the son of Mary…?" (6:3). They cannot understand why people are making such a fuss over him. Herod says, "John the baptizer has been raised from the dead…" (6:14). Mark records all of these opinions. And more oddly, the only ones who correctly identify Jesus in the first half of Mark are the devils (5:17)!

"You Are the Christ"

We do not hear from the disciples until Peter's profession at Caesarea Philippi, because Jesus does not allow them to address the question of his identity.[3] Rather, he lets them observe what he is doing. But at last, Jesus takes his disciples away from the crowd and asks, "Who do people say that I am?…Who do you say that I am?"

Peter says, "You are the Messiah" (8:29).

We tend to interpret Peter's understanding of *the Christ* in terms of Israel's history. The Jews considered themselves to be God's chosen nation, who had been promised a Messiah to deliver them from their oppressors. So when Peter declares that Jesus is "the Messiah," we suppose he means that Jesus is the divine Deliverer, the culmination of the long historical process that God had initiated for the Jews.

But if we take Mark seriously, we must draw a different conclusion. In light of the repeated demonstrations of Jesus' adequacy for every human need, Peter must not mean, "You are the one Israel has been looking for." Rather, he must mean, "You are the one the entire world has been looking for." Christ was not primarily the fulfillment of a national dream, but the fulfillment of a universal hope; not primarily the culmination of a divinely ordained process, but the answer to human need. For those who have questions,

Jesus is the Truth. For those who are sick, Jesus is Health. For those who are alienated, Jesus is the Restorer of relationships. Peter is saying, "Jesus, you are the One everyone has been looking for. You can meet all of our needs."

Unless we perceive that we have a need, we cannot experience a relationship with Jesus as the Christ. A self-sufficient person cannot discern who Jesus is. But the paralytic, the woman with the issue of blood, the man with a dying daughter—all could know Jesus as the Christ. Their need gave Jesus an opportunity to demonstrate who he is. We see this connection between need and revelation in each of Mark's accounts of miraculous healing.

If people suppose they have no need, they will prevent Jesus from manifesting himself. For this reason, when I step into the pulpit to preach, I pray, "Lord, let some folks in this crowd realize their need." Jesus can enter a person's life when he authenticates himself by meeting a need that is already there.

Mark recounts these stories of human need as his own way of saying "All have sinned and fall short of the glory of God" (Rom. 3:23). What Paul says propositionally, Mark says experientially. When a person comes to realize that Jesus is the Christ—i.e., the One every person needs—he will either trust Jesus and be saved, or reject him and be depraved. Each person must align himself with the truth or step into a world of delusion, which is the only option that sinfulness can afford.

"You Do Not Think as God Thinks"

So the universal adequacy of Jesus is the theme that occupies the first eight chapters of Mark. But another important theme begins to emerge there, a theme that will be the focus of the concluding chapters, and the real crux of our study. That theme is *the impact that Jesus has upon a person's understanding.*

We catch a glimpse of this theme at Jesus' miracle of feeding the five thousand, where Jesus scolds his disciples, saying, "Beware of the yeast of the Pharisees" (8:15). They think he is upset because they do not have enough bread to feed the multitude, but he is referring the perverted thinking of the carnal mind. "Do you still not perceive or understand?" he asks (8:17).

They come to Bethsaida, where the people beg him to heal a blind man. Jesus touches him and asks, "Can you see anything?" The man replies, "I can see people; but they look like trees, walking" (8:24). So Jesus touches him again, and the man says that he sees things clearly now (8:25). Jesus warns him not to go into the village or tell anyone what has happened; it is to be strictly between the two of them.

Jesus and his disciples continue toward the villages of Caesarea Philippi. Along the way, Peter declares that Jesus is the Christ. The minute Jesus knows that they have perceived who he is, he begins to teach them that he must suffer. The disciples know he is the King, and they want to say, "Glory!" But Jesus seems to say, "No, that's the wrong word for what I'm about to do. I'm going up to Jerusalem to suffer!" They want to put him on a throne, but he knows he is going to a cross.

Peter takes Jesus aside and begins to rebuke him. In one breath, he says Jesus is the long-awaited Messiah; in the next, he lectures Jesus on messianic theology. Jesus rebukes Peter, saying, "Get behind me, Satan!" (8:33).[4] Jesus' followers are eager to tell him an easier way to accomplish his will; but he calls them to think as he does, to view each situation with his priorities in mind. When a person does that, he will respond to problems much differently than the human mind bent on self-preservation.

I now consider Jesus' reprimand of Peter to be the prime biblical text for holiness of heart: "You think as men think, not as God thinks" (Mark 8:33, NEB). The Greek literally means, "You are not minded as God is minded." "You do not think as God thinks."

"He called the crowd with his disciples, and said to them, 'If any want to become my followers, let them deny themselves and take up their cross and follow me'" (8:34). Note that suffering is the context of discipleship, the backdrop of Jesus' call to "Follow me." Jesus is saying, "Follow me. I'm going to the cross!" He is headed for Jerusalem and the ultimate self-sacrifice. Anyone who wishes to follow Jesus has to be willing to sacrifice himself as well, to endure the hardships of obedience to the will of God. As the missionary Amy Carmichael once wrote,

> Can he have followed far
> Who has no wound nor scar?

So much Christian evangelism calls people to receive things from God. Indeed, we are called to receive the gift of salvation; but in every other sense we are called to give. Jesus' call is to self-sacrifice. "For those who want to save their life will lose it, and those who lose their life for my sake, and for the sake of the gospel, will save it" Jesus says (Mark 8:35).

The next major event in Mark's Gospel is the transfiguration of Jesus (9:2ff.). On the Mount of Transfiguration, the faith that said, "You are the Messiah," becomes knowledge; for here Peter, James, and John listen to Moses and Elijah talking with Jesus "about his departure" (Luke 9:31). Note that the Greek word here translated as "departure" is *exodon*, from which we get the word *Exodus*. You will recall that the Exodus in the Old Testament was the event in which the people of God were born. Likewise, in the New Testament, the passion of Christ is the event in which the people of God are born; his crucifixion and resurrection are the Exodus of the church.

As Jesus and his disciples descend from the mountain, Jesus warns them to tell no one what has happened until he has risen from the dead (Mark 9:9). This perplexes them. They cannot understand what Jesus means by "rising from the dead," because they still do not think as he thinks.

Spiritual Dissipation and Clamor for Status

When they reach the foot of the hill, they encounter a crowd that is teeming with commotion. Jesus steps into the midst of the crowd and asks what is wrong. A distraught father pushes his way to Jesus and says, "I brought you my son; he has a spirit that makes him unable to speak;...I asked your disciples to cast it out, but they were unable to do so" (Mark 9:17-18).

Just a few days earlier, the disciples had traveled through the countryside, casting out demons. Now that they have begun congratulating themselves and contradicting the Lord himself, they are perplexed by this man's need. So it is with every disciple of the Lord: When we think of how spiritually strong we are, we cannot maintain our spiritual strength. Instead of going from victory to victory, we go from dissipation to dissipation. The pastoral ministry is loaded with people who once knew more of God than they do today. Clearly, it is possible to slip out of intimate fellowship with the Master.

The disciples ask Jesus why they were unable to cast out the demons, and he replies, "You faithless generation (literally, "short-of-faith generation"), how much longer must I be among you?" (v. 19). Faith is an expression of our inability; as we feel more self-confident and self-adequate, we lose faith in the Lord.

Jesus confirms this by saying, "This kind can come out only through prayer" (v. 29). Prayer is an expression of dependence on God. The moment that the disciples believe that they have a franchise on spiritual power, they lose it! Because they had been able to exorcize demons, they feel no need to pray; they suppose they can simply command miracles to happen. The work a Christian disciple is called to do can be accomplished only by the Lord. But a self-reliant disciple gets only what he himself can do.

Next the Gospel writer tells us, "They went on from there and passed through Galilee. He did not want anyone to know it" (9:30). Jesus shuts himself up with his disciples so that he can teach them about his impending death and resurrection. He gives them a walking seminar on the cross. "But they did not understand what he was saying and were afraid to ask him" (Mark 9:32). They do not wish to appear stupid.

The group comes to Capernaum and enters "the house" (v. 33)— apparently, the place where Jesus had lived for the past three and a half years. Jesus asks them, "What were you arguing about on the way?"

The disciples are silent, for they have been discussing which of them will be the greatest disciple. So Jesus calls the disciples close to him and explains, "Whoever wants to be first must be last of all and servant of all" (v. 35). He takes a child in his arms and says, "Whosoever welcomes one such child in my name welcomes me; and whoever welcomes me welcomes not me but him who sent me" (v. 37). Why does he choose a child to illustrate this truth? We normally suppose he does it because of the child's transparent honesty, naivete, and openness; but I think he does it because the child has no status. The disciples want to be the greatest; so Jesus makes a child their example.

The status-less people of our world are the best models of Christian lifestyle. Mother Teresa of Calcutta demonstrated this in her mission work. The people of India are impressed with position and status. But Mother Teresa lavished her attention on the homeless and the outcasts, because they are best prepared to live as Christ calls us to live. Jesus "did not regard equality with God as something to be exploited, but emptied himself, taking the form of a slave" (Phil. 2:6-7). He was not captive to status. If we wish to be like Jesus, we are called to be like that.

The disciples are feeling a bit chagrined, so John speaks up. "Teacher, we saw someone casting out demons in your name, and we tried to stop him, because he was not following us" (Mark 9:38). How ironic! The disciples have just had an experience in which they could not cast out demons; so when they find a man who can, they forbid him from doing it! Jesus has just been talking about the problem of status, yet the disciples are concerned with ministerial status. They are disturbed by a man who has apostolic power without being one of the apostles. So Jesus replies, "Do not stop him; for no one who does a deed of power in my name will be able soon afterward to speak evil of me. Whoever is not against us is for us" (9:39-40).

Shortly after this, the people bring children to Jesus that he might touch them, and the disciples rebuke them. They think Jesus has no time for children. (They must not have been paying attention to what Jesus had just done and said!) But Jesus says again, "Let the little children come to me, do not stop them; for it is to such as these that the kingdom of God belongs" (10:14). The disciples are looking for Christ's Kingdom, but they have a different notion of the Kingdom than he has. So Jesus repeats the message: "Truly I tell you, whoever does not receive the kingdom of God as a little child will never enter it" (v. 15). Jesus takes the children in his arms and blesses them.

Jesus continues his march toward Jerusalem with his disciples trailing along behind, "And the disciples were perplexed at these words" (10:24). The Greek word is *thambeō*, literally meaning, "They were trembling and astounded." Why? Because Jesus tells them what is about to happen.

> See, we are going up to Jerusalem; and the Son of Man will be handed over to the chief priests and the scribes, and they will condemn him to death; then they will hand him over to the Gentiles; they will mock him, and spit upon him, and flog him, and kill him; and after three days he will rise again (9:33-34).

Mark makes no further comment about this conversation; but I imagine Peter and John look at each other, shrug their shoulders, and say, "There he goes again! He has to recite this litany every time we turn toward Jerusalem. We can't feature what he means; but if he feels better saying it, let him say it." They have no comprehension of what he is saying.

The disciples suppose they are protégé prophets, as Elisha was to Elijah. They are eager to inherit the power and authority of their Master. They do not expect that their Master will be executed when he goes to Jerusalem; nor do they expect to be executed themselves.

James and John approach him and say, "Teacher, we want you to do for us whatever we ask of you" (9:35). They exercise the currently fashionable theology that says, "Name it and claim it." So what do they want? "Grant us to sit, one at your right hand and one at your left, in your glory." They know his glory is coming; after all, he is the

Christ. But Jesus says, "You do not know what you are asking. Are you able to drink the cup that I drink, or be baptized with the baptism that I am to be baptized with?" (10:38).

James and John blurt out, "We are able."

Jesus says, "The cup that I drink you will drink; and with the baptism with which I am baptized, you will be baptized; but to sit at the right hand or at my left is not mine to grant, but it is for those for whom it has been prepared" (vv. 39-40).

When the other ten disciples hear this exchange, they are angry with James and John. They too want to sit at Jesus' right and left. So Jesus explains further:

> You know that among the Gentiles those whom they recognize as their rulers lord it over them, and their great ones are tyrants over them. But it is not so among you; but whoever wishes to become great among you must be your servant, and whoever wishes to be first among you must be slave of all. For the Son of Man came not to be served but to serve, and to give his life a ransom for many (vv. 42-45).

The next chapters detail Jesus' triumphal entry into Jerusalem. In chapter 14, Jesus predicts that all of the disciples will forsake him (v. 27). Two verses later, Peter denies that he will. Two verse after that, the other eleven deny that they will. And nineteen verses following that, the Bible says, "They all forsook him and fled." In the courtyard, Peter denies that he ever knew Jesus (14:66-72).

From Peter's confession at Caesarea Philippi until the end of Mark, we read no good thing about the Twelve. That is no coincidence. The first half of Mark reveals who Jesus is; the last half reveals who we are. It is picture of human nature in its common form, tainted with self-interest and lust for status.

Notice that these problems of spiritual dissipation and the clamor for status nevertheless emerge in intimate fellowship with Jesus and with other disciples. A person does not realize this self-centered bent so long as he lives in isolation. One needs to live in community to realize the problems in his own soul.

I am convinced this need for Christian community was the motive behind John Wesley's creation of bands and classes in early

Methodism. I do not think there was a better way to teach holiness. The class meetings revealed one's own carnality and the tyranny of one's self-interest. We usually consider the church to be a place for edification, for building up one another in the faith; but it is also a place for examination and self-disclosure. That is a painful part of church life which we do not like; but it is a necessary part. On the foreign mission field, the mission workers' greatest problems are not with the unsaved, but with the other missionaries. That is part of the divine plan. As we serve together in the Kingdom, we learn who we are.

Theology Shaped in Relationships

Our theology is shaped in personal relationships. Mark emphasizes this fact by noting the *names* of the leading characters in the latter half of his Gospel. The other Gospels seldom give the names of people involved in Jesus' ministry; but in Mark, the personal names abound:

- It is *Peter* who confesses that Jesus is the Christ.
- It is *Peter, James,* and *John* who do not understand what "rising from the dead" means.
- It is *James* and *John* who want to sit at Jesus' right hand and left.
- It is *John* who says the disciples forbade a man from casting out demons in Jesus' name.
- It is *Peter* who says, "I will never forsake you."
- It is *Peter, James,* and *John* who go to sleep in the Garden of Gethsemane.
- And it is *Peter* who denies Jesus three times.

The irony of this list is that Mark supposedly got his data from Peter. Tradition says that Mark was Peter's understudy. Had Mark wanted to be charitable to Peter, he could have imitated John's method, referring to Peter as "one of the disciples." But there is no cover-up of Peter's foibles in this book. I believe Mark is making a strong affirmation of the defective flaw of human nature. In the Book of Acts, Peter is foremost among the leaders; in the Gospel of Mark, he is the worst example of human failure. Mark seems to be saying, "I want you to realize that the best of us is no better than the worst of us. We are all alike. Our champions are as carnal as our traitors." Again, it is Mark's way of saying that all have sinned and come short of the glory of God. There is a godless bent in all of us.[5]

From Mark to Acts

The Gospel of Mark closes with a very discouraging picture of human nature. If one were to preach the gospel based solely on Mark, one could express little hope for human improvement. But the resurrection and ascension of Jesus, which close Mark's Gospel, are not the end of the story.

First, Acts 1-5 portrays how Jesus' disciples, who had been unable to think the way he thought, are transformed completely, even in their thinking. Peter begins his sermon on the Day of Pentecost by telling the crowd, "Let this be known to you" (Acts 2:14). Their spiritual insight is awakened by the experience they have had that day. One of the inevitable consequences of receiving the Holy Spirit is spiritual understanding. (George Mueller said that, on the night he was filled with the Holy Spirit, he learned more in four hours about the Word of God than he had understood in the previous four years of his preaching from it.)

Second, the Book of Acts records how the disciples regained their lost spiritual power. At the end of Mark, they are unable to heal a demon-possessed boy; but in Acts, they can say to a cripple, "In the name of Jesus Christ of Nazareth, stand up and walk" (Acts 3:6).

Third, the Book of Acts shows that the disciples shook off the tyranny of self-interest. They are brought to trial before the Sanhedrin, which forbids them to preach about Jesus, and they reply, "We must obey God rather than any human authority" (Acts 5:29). They are no longer concerned with their status.

Every negative quality of the Twelve reported in the latter half of Mark is reversed in the Book of Acts. What does it? A baptism of fire—the baptism of the Holy Spirit, who cleanses them of all these things.

The three laws of Christian discipleship are: (1) Find out who Jesus is. Learn his adequacy for every human need. (2) Find out who you are. Realize your inadequacy for serving in God's Kingdom, no matter how earnestly you try. (3) Find the Holy Spirit's power to displace your human weakness with the fullness of Christ. When we do these things, we begin to think differently; we have different emotions; our entire outlook is changed.

We do not see all three steps of this sequence in the Gospel of Mark, for it is a signpost book that points us to the Book of Acts, where Christians began to experience the Holy Spirit's transforming power. The essence of Mark is summarized in Jesus' statement of Mark 8:33, where he says in effect, "You do not think the way God thinks." Not until the disciples received the baptism of the Holy Spirit would they be delivered from the enslavement of self-interest, the hallmark of the natural mind.

Endnotes

[1] Some are now asserting that miraculous signs and wonders must accompany God's people, but that is not the typical way in which God manifests himself. Jeremiah had the longest ministry of any prophet in the Old Testament, yet he never performed a miracle. When Jesus asked his disciples, "Who do people say that I am?" They replied, "Some say...Jeremiah or one of the prophets" (Matt. 16:14). What accounted for the similarity between Jeremiah and Jesus? Not their signs and wonders, but their moral authenticity. Christians today do not need to perform signs and wonders to be like Jesus, for that is not the essence of who Jesus is.

[2] The devils of hell have all the knowledge of Scripture at their disposal, but it has not saved one of them. Nor can it save us. We moderns live under the illusion that knowledge will save us from all of our problems; but only faith can put us in touch with the One who can do that. Faith is a personal relationship with the Savior, Jesus Christ.

[3] A capable teacher does not ask questions too soon; and the teacher is better served if the first answer is wrong! The last thing a teacher wants is a bright fellow sitting on the front row, ready to answer every question; that stymies all learning.

[4] These are the strongest words Jesus ever used in personal conversation; he never called a Pharisee "Satan." But he calls Peter this, because Peter is speaking Satan's lines! Satan had told Jesus this sort of thing before, when he said there was a way Jesus could win the world without going to the Cross (Matt. 4:9). But the Lord recognized these lies for what they were.

[5] Mark mentions an unnamed young man who fled from Jesus' enemies in Gethsemane, leaving his clothes behind (14:51-52). Tradition says this was Mark himself. If so, Mark is saying that he himself was as self-centered as the rest.

5

The Carnal Mind vs. The Mind of Christ

Do you feel there is a tug-of-war going on within you? Do you find yourself hesitating to do what God is calling you to do, because you feel there might be a more pleasant or more socially acceptable alternative? Do you feel guilty because you hold back from giving yourself fully to the Lord?

The divided heart is an agonizing state to live in. It's impossible for a person to stay there long; you will choose either God's way or the world's way. I've observed that the divided heart is a common experience among Christians. However, it is not the way that the New Testament calls us to live.

Romans 8 says, "There is therefore now no condemnation for those who are in Christ Jesus. For the law of the Spirit of life in Christ Jesus has set you free from the law of sin and of death. For God has done what the law, weakened by the flesh, could not do: by sending his own Son in the likeness of sinful flesh, and to deal with sin, he condemned sin in the flesh, so that the just requirement of the law might be fulfilled in us, who walk not according to the flesh but according to the Spirit" (vv. 1-4). Paul says the requirements of God's law can be fulfilled in the likes of you and me. He says the power of God can bring us to the point that we can please God himself.

Paul acknowledges that there are two ways people can attempt to please God. One way is to work out of our own resources. The other is to let God put his Spirit in us and fill us, so that we can live out of the resources of the Spirit. If we attempt to live out of our own resources, Paul says, we're living "according to the flesh." But if we live out of the resources of God, we live "according to the Spirit." Paul sees no third alternative. Ultimately, you and I must live one way or the other. We must live "in the flesh" without God or we must live in the Spirit and be totally God's.

I am intrigued by the sharp contrast that Paul draws between the "flesh" and the Spirit. He makes very clear the disastrous consequences of living "in the flesh" and the glorious privileges of living in the Spirit. Notice what he says about living in "the flesh."

First, he says is that if you live "in the flesh," you will die. Verse 6 bluntly declares that "to set the mind (Gk., *phroneō*) on the flesh is death." Verse 13 reiterates, "If you live according to the flesh, you will die." Why? Because life is in God; it is not in us. So if we attempt to live in our own power and wisdom, we will perish.

Second, he says that if you try to live without God, you will be hostile to God. No one can remain neutral with regard to God's will. Notice verse 7: "For this reason the mind that is set on the flesh is hostile to God; it does not submit to God's law—indeed it cannot." Apart from the Holy Spirit's working in a person's life, that person will be hostile to God. The flesh sees God as the enemy. The perfect picture of demonstration of that fact is the Cross, where the likes of you and me murdered God when he came to live among us. Paul is setting up the sharply etched reality that there can be no middle ground between life "in the flesh" and life in the Spirit.

Third, he says is that if you live "in the flesh," you cannot please God. Notice verse 8: "Those who are in the flesh cannot please God." So if human desire dominates my life, I will find a hostility rising in me against God. I will not please him. I will be separated from him. I have no option but death.

The fourth thing Paul says is that living "in the flesh" is to live in bondage. Look at verse 15: "For you did not receive the spirit of slavery to fall back into fear, but you have received a spirit of adoption." He's contrasting the Spirit of God and the spirit of human flesh, saying that the flesh is bondage. The natural man knows what it means to live in bondage. It may be a habit; it may be lust; it may be any manifestation of sin. Whatever form the bondage may take, a human being living in the flesh is powerless to rid himself of sin. That bondage brings an ominous sense of fear. We know intuitively that we are not right, so we have a fear of God.

Life in the Spirit

Now Paul shows us the opposite. "For the law of the Spirit of life in Christ Jesus has set you free from the law of sin and of death" (v. 2). Sin does not have to dominate us. Death does not have to determine our destiny. In fact, if you look at verse 4, you will even find that it is possible for a person like you and me to please God. The end result in verse 6 is that we have life and peace. We have the privilege of being led by the Holy Spirit. We can walk in the Spirit. We don't have to fear God, because he puts a witness in our heart that we are his children and we belong to him. What an incredible experience it is when God tells you that you belong to him!

Then, as we walk with him, the Holy Spirit intercedes on our behalf. Look at verse 26: "Likewise the Spirit helps us in our weakness; for we do not know how to pray as we ought, but that very Spirit intercedes with sighs too deep for words." We don't even know what to pray for. So the Holy Spirit prays for us, with sighs too deep for words. The Spirit intercedes for us according to the will of the Father; it is the Father's will that the Spirit states our case. What a marvelous privilege it is, to have the Holy Spirit pleading on our behalf before the throne of heaven!

So Paul sees only two ways to live—in the flesh or in the Holy Spirit. One is a life without God and the other is a life with all the resources of God. The problem is that most of us Christians have known very well how it feels to have a mixture of the two within us. Most of us have tried to live part of our lives—perhaps most of our lives—in a kind of spiritually comatose state. There has not been a clear separation between "flesh" and Spirit. We have been neither fully alive nor dead.

If we are to stand before God, our hearts must be cleansed of this double-mindedness. God must make us holy so that we will be wholly his. There can be no divided loyalties in the Kingdom of God. If you read the biographies of great Christian leaders, you will find how this battle has been fought in their lives.

I remember reading the story of Albert Orsburn, one of the early leaders of the Salvation Army. Orsburn was the great poet and hymn writer of the Salvation Army. In his early ministry, he had been made commander over a district in the city of London. He had an excellent district and God began to work profoundly among his soldiers. Revival began to break out in the different segments of the Army under his control. Sinners were converted and numbers were being added to their group. Then one day, one of his officers came to him and said, "I have heard a rumor that the brass are going to divide our district." The officer said, "We can't let this happen. God is blessing us so much. If they divide our district, it will hinder the work of God. I think you ought to fight it."

"Oh, no," Orsburn said. "I want to do the will of God and respect my superiors. I will not do that."

Soon his superiors called him in and told him that they indeed planned to divide his district. He said he suddenly found an attitude in his heart that he didn't want. He knew that if they divided that district, his position would not be as prestigious as it was at present. He would not have as much power as before. So he began to argue with his superiors. Looking back on it later, he said, "Unwittingly, I had begun to fight, not for the Kingdom, but for my position in the Kingdom. And the Holy Spirit was grieved."

I will never forget the tone in Orsburn's voice as he told this story. He said, "When the Spirit grieves, the Spirit leaves."

He was a Salvation Army officer, so he managed to keep going through the motions; yet there was a strange distance between Orsburn and God now. A coldness began to move over his spirit. An indifference and a hardness of spirit came. He kept on doing the same thing, but he knew there was an emptiness inside.

Then he was in an automobile accident. He said, "I ended up in the hospital and was a long time in recovery. The gracious Holy Spirit began to deal with my heart once again. One day I heard some singing next door. As I heard them sing of the glories of God, my heart began to yearn again to have that kind of intimacy with God. I wept my heart out in repentance. God forgave me, and the Spirit came and filled my heart afresh."

As a result, Orsburn sat down and wrote a new hymn. He wrote: "Savior, if my feet have faltered on the pathway of the Cross,/If my purposes have altered or my gold be mixed with dross,/O forbid me not Thy service, keep me yet in Thy employ,/Pass me through a sterner cleansing if I may but give Thee joy!"[1]

Here was a man who had known God and did not want to lose him; but he knew there was something in his heart separating him from God. Now in penitence he said, "Lord, can you take this rebellious attitude out of me, so that there is an unbroken relationship and I can once again live in the Spirit?"

Why the Hostility?

Why is the Holy Spirit so hostile to what the Scripture calls "the flesh"? Because the flesh is never profitable for anything eternal.

I want to tell you a story that was told to me by an old American preacher, who was giving a series of lectures at Asbury Seminary when I was a student there. One day I was his host and found myself sitting, talking with him. He spoke to me about the man who had been the founder of Asbury Theological Seminary, Henry Clay Morrison. Morrison was one of the greatest preachers in America.

My guest said that he and Morrison once were preaching together in a camp meeting. On Sunday morning, my friend had to preach. A twinkle came to his eye as he said, "Son, there are days when a man preaches better than he is capable of preaching. That day the Holy Spirit descended on me and we had an incredible service. There was a glorious response of sinners seeking God. That night,

Dr. Morrison began preaching on Moses' giving the law on Mt. Sinai. Morrison was a great orator. But the longer he preached, the more a little suspicion began to grow inside me. I thought, *We had a great service this morning. Morrison is not used to being with anyone who preaches better than he does. So he thinks that tonight we must have a greater service."*

Finally, the service ended and everyone went to their tents. My guest crawled into his cot and the lights began to go out on the campground. The sounds stopped and everything was very still. Suddenly, my friend heard something rustling in the grass outside his tent. He realized that someone was pulling back the opening of his tent and coming inside. He wondered who it was. The intruder stumbled around until he found the foot of his bed. He knelt in the foot of the preacher's bed, buried his face in the covers over his feet, and began to sob as if his heart would break. He suddenly knew it was the great preacher, Henry Clay Morrison. Neither man said a word. Spirit spoke to spirit.

Then the visiting preacher turned and said to me, "Young man, Henry Clay Morrison was one of the most famous men in the Christian world. But he had gotten into the flesh and he had preached for the sake of his own appearances rather than the glory of God. The Holy Spirit quickened his conscience and convicted him of the sin of it. He could not sleep until he had found his friend and acknowledged his sin."

I'm glad Henry Clay Morrison had that kind of sensitivity to the Holy Spirit, because I found Christ as a result of the ministry of that man. My wife also found Christ under the ministry of Henry Clay Morrison.

There is power when we live in the Spirit. There are only sterility and death in the works of the flesh.

The Body of Christ has never learned that. We still squabble for position. We fight for power. We want what we want, when we want it. We try to sanctify our desires by saying, "This is for God." But our motives are mixed. We have a double mind. As a result, our works are sterile. Oh, how we need to have the mind of Christ!

Only when we have his mind and live his way can the fullness of the Spirit of God flow through us and be manifest in our living and in our service.

The Carnal Mind vs. The Mind of Christ

You may think that the phrase "carnal mind" is a bit old-fashioned. Perhaps it is. But it is thoroughly biblical. Whether we use the term or not, we certainly need to understand the truth that Scripture sets before us when it speaks of the "carnal mind." Nowhere is that more obvious than in Romans 8.

Take another look at what Paul says: "For those who live according to the flesh set their minds (Gk., *phroneō*) on things of the flesh, but those who live according to the Spirit set their minds on the things of the Spirit" (v. 5). There again is that flag word, *phroneō*. Remember that it speaks of a person's entire perspective on life—what one thinks, feels, and aspires to do. Paul is saying that a carnally-minded person is driven by physical desires. The appetites rule. Such a person seeks whatever brings pleasure, whatever "feels good."

In contrast to that is the person who thinks with the mind of Christ. This person has the perspective of Christ's own Spirit. This person seeks whatever pleases the Spirit of the Lord. This person yearns to know where Christ's Spirit is at work, and join in that work. The person who sets his mind on the Spirit of Christ sees the world through Christ's eyes and seeks to be a part of what he is doing in the world.

John Wesley referred to this way of thinking as "Christian perfection." Notice what he says in his journal entry for January 27, 1767:

> …By perfection, I mean the humble, gentle, patient love of God, and our neighbor, ruling our tempers, words, and actions. I do not include an impossibility of falling from it, either in part or in whole. Therefore, I retract several expressions in our Hymns, which partly express, partly imply, such an impossibility…. I believe this perfection is always wrought in the soul by a simple act of faith; consequently, in an instant.

> But I believe [there is] a gradual work, both preceding and fol-
> lowing that instant.... As to the time[,] I believe this instant
> generally is the instant of death, the moment before the soul
> leaves the body. But I believe it may be ten, twenty, or forty
> years before. I believe it is usually many years after justifica-
> tion, but it might be within five years or five months after it;
> I know of no conclusive argument to the contrary.[2]

It's unfortunate that so many people have a distorted view of what Wesley meant by "perfection." He makes it clear that he is talk-ing about the same thing that Paul describes in Romans 8. This is not an experience for a spiritual elite corps; it is God's gift for all of his children. It is a gift that we may not receive till long after our conversion. Indeed, some of us don't receive it until the moment of death. But that doesn't change the fact that life in the Spirit is offered to all of God's people. None of us need to serve our human passions. "We are debtors, not to the flesh, to live according to the flesh" (Rom. 8:12), but rather to serve God in the Spirit of his Son, Jesus Christ.

"My Father Is So Pleased"

I met a very winsome young man from Latin America. His father was a professional man. The young man became a Christian at about the age of twenty. He became a very passionate follower of Christ. Within a year after his conversion, he led about sixty other young persons to Christ. I asked him what his ambition was. He said, "My ambition is to be a pastor in Latin America."

Now the evangelical church in Latin America is not well-respected, and not many young people want to be evangelical pastors there. When this young man told his father that he planned to be the pastor of a church, his father was horrified. But the young man said, "God has saved me. I want to serve him. I want to be pastor of a church, regardless of the social status it brings."

He came to the United States to get a Christian education. I met him a year or two after he arrived at an evangelical Christian col-lege. I asked, "How is your work going?"

"Oh," he said, "now I am majoring in psychology. I am training to be a psychiatrist and a counselor. My father is so pleased!" This young man, who at one stage was listening to the call of Christ, now for appearances' sake was conforming to the patterns of his unbelieving father and family.

So many of us allow our conduct to be affected by the world around us. We try to please the Lord and please the world at the same time, but Paul says that's impossible.

Paul says we need to stand up against the standards of our worldly culture. We must oppose even the value systems of many of our fellow Christians. We must put ourselves in the places where people need to be touched by Jesus Christ. That means we must go into some very unsavory places, for that is where people need him the most.

God is looking for people who will keep traveling down "the Roman road" from salvation to live as Christ lives. That kind of life takes more than courage. It takes more than insight. It takes the very Spirit of Christ, living within us and animating our lives every day.

Endnotes

[1]Albert Orsborn, "All My Work Is For the Master," *The Song Book of the Salvation Army* (Verona, N.J.: The Salvation Army, 1986) p. 473.

[2]Thomas Jackson, ed., *The Works of Wesley*, Vol. XI (Grand Rapids: Zondervan Publishing House, n.d.), p. 446.

6

From Middle Ground to Higher Ground

Imagine you are reporting for the first day of a new job assignment. Your supervisor hands you a typewritten page and says, "Here's your revised job description." You scan the page and realize with horror that you are woefully unqualified for the duties you are expected to handle. How do you respond?

You could politely excuse yourself and ask for your old job back. You could try to bluff your way through, hoping that no one will discover your shortcomings. You could protest what your supervisor expects you to do. Or you could admit your deficiency and ask for help. Regardless of the approach you take, there's no doubt you are in an awkward spot.

In a sense, that's where the Christians at Corinth were when they began to read Paul's first epistle to them. He said he was writing to the whole church at Corinth, people that he said were "called to be saints" (1 Cor. 1:2).

Now Paul knows the Corinthians very well. He had led many of them to the Lord, so he is well aware that they were still new to the Christian faith. He knows their church is racked with dissention and immorality. He planned to send his protégé Timothy to try to restore unity among them. Even though he knows all of this, he names them "sanctified" people who are "called to be saints." How could they possibly live up to that?

We need to answer that question too, because the letter is also addressed to us. Paul says he is writing to "all those who in every place call on the name of our Lord Jesus Christ" (v. 2). That's you and me. How can we hope to be "sanctified" people, who live as "saints" in this world?

Our first impulse is to question Paul's terminology. He says we are supposed to be "sanctified" (Gk., *hagiosmenois*) and "saints" (Gk., *hagiois*), both of which come from the Greek word for "holy" (*hagios*). Exactly what does he mean?

In ancient Greece, *hagios* was strictly a religious term, denoting something that was worthy of God's presence. God told Moses to take off his sandals at the burning bush because he stood on "holy ground" (Acts 7:33). Peter called the Mount of Transfiguration "the holy mountain" (2 Pet. 1:18). Jerusalem was called the "holy city" (Matt. 4:5). The Temple was called a "holy place" (Matt. 24:15; Acts 6:13). In each case, the Bible uses this specialized Greek word, *hagios.*

The word *hagios* could be applied to persons as well. "Holy" people were consecrated to God's service. In this sense, the Old Testament prophets were "holy" (Luke 1:70; Acts 3:21) and the apostles were "holy" (Eph. 3:5). They had dedicated themselves to serve God alone.

Several passages of the New Testament further indicate that "holy" people are to behave differently than others. They are to live more wisely than the rest of society. They are not to yield to the impulses and desires that people normally obey. So Peter says, "Like obedient children, do not be conformed to the desires that you formerly had in ignorance. Instead, as he who called you is holy, be holy yourselves in all your conduct" (1 Pet. 1:14-16). "And you who were once estranged and hostile in mind, doing evil deeds," Paul says, "he has now reconciled in his fleshly body through death, so as to present you holy and blameless and irreproachable before him" (Col. 1:21-22).

The word study doesn't make our calling sound any easier, does it? If anything, the deeper we delve into the particulars of what it means to be "sanctified" people, the less qualified we find ourselves to be. In fact, the Bible says that as "holy" people, we are supposed to live in this world as Jesus Christ lived. How is it possible for anyone but Jesus himself to do that?

Coming to grips with the truth of Scripture can be frightening. I recently had a conversation with a layman who had just finished his tenure as the head of United Methodist Men in the state of Georgia. I said, "Tell me, how did you become a Christian?"

"Well, I grew up in a Baptist home and I found Christ early in life," he said. " Then I became a football player. That is a different world, of course, and I kind of pushed Christ to the margin of my life. I got married and soon we had a baby. The baby had a hole in her heart. For a couple of weeks there, we didn't know if she was going to survive. So I found myself sitting in the hospital every night until 1:30 in the morning, patting that little baby's arm and hoping that she was going to live.

"One night as I came out of the hospital room, walking down a dark passage way, I noticed a light shining from an open door. I turned to see what it was and found that I was in a chapel. I just slipped inside and sat down. I found there was a Bible, so I opened it and began to read. The thing I started reading was John 15, where Jesus says, 'I am the vine, you are the branches. If you don't abide in me, you will be cast off and burned.'"

He said, "I read that and a profound terror swept over me. It was as if my life insurance policy had just been canceled."

In that moment, this young man realized that the Bible does not teach "once in grace, always in grace." He had drifted away from the Lord. If he remained cut off from the Lord, he would die. That honest confrontation with the Word began to turn his life around.

I suspect the Corinthians had a similar experience when they began reading this letter from Paul. He was confronting them with a calling that they were completely unqualified to fill. Yet they could not evade what he was saying. They could not quibble about terms. His meaning was absolutely clear: God expects his people to be different from the rest of the world. He expects us to be like him.

A Good Beginning

Paul praised the Christians at Corinth because they had made a good beginning. "I give thanks to my God always for you," he said, "because of the grace of God that has been given you in Christ Jesus" (1 Cor. 1:4). They had been converted. Through the saving grace of Jesus Christ, they had been "born again." They were regenerated, raised from the deadness of sin to the new life of being in Christ. They were justified, as Christ took responsibility for their sin before the Great Judge of the universe.

Second, he said, "You have been enriched in him, in speech and knowledge of every kind" (1 Cor. 1:5). The Corinthians had learned a great deal of spiritual truth and they knew how to communicate it to others. They knew the gospel story and they could tell it persuasively to others.

This is why Paul said, third, "The testimony of Christ has been strengthened in your midst" (1 Cor. 1:6). The Corinthians publicly identified themselves as Christians. They weren't shy about telling their pagan neighbors that they were followers of Jesus Christ.

Fourth, Paul said, "You are not lacking in any spiritual gift" (1 Cor. 1:7). They possessed and exercised every God-given ability that a church might need. In fact, Paul describes their gifts in great detail later in this letter, and the variety of their gifts is impressive indeed.

Fifth, "You are waiting for the revealing of our Lord Jesus Christ" (1 Cor. 1:7). They lived in eager anticipation that the Lord would soon return. They were a community of hope and expectancy. They looked to the future with bright eyes of joy, because they knew their Lord was coming to gather them to himself.

What a marvelous beginning the Corinthians had made! If only we could say these things of all congregations today! Yet there were signs of trouble in their midst.

Turmoil in the Church

Despite Paul's glowing words of praise for his friends in Corinth, he saw their turmoil as well. "There are quarrels among you, my brothers and sisters," Paul said (1 Cor. 1:11). They were torn by doctrinal factions (1 Cor. 1:11-17). They vaunted themselves over one another, claiming to be more wise or more spiritually mature that one another (1 Cor. 1:18-25). "It is actually reported that there is sexual immorality among you," Paul groaned (1 Cor. 5:1), and he went on to describe a sordid case of incest. The members of the church were taking each other to court, charging fraud and corruption (1 Cor. 6:1-8). They condemned one another for their beliefs on celibacy (1 Cor. 7:25-39), eating food that had been purchased from pagan temples (1 Cor. 8), whether women should cover their heads in worship services (1 Cor. 11:2-16), and a host of other issues. How could any group of Christian people dissolve into such a bickering mob?

Sadly, anyone who has been associated with any congregation for very long knows only too well how this can happen. People just do "what comes naturally." Our human natures are inclined to indulge in arrogance, jealousy, egotism, and contentiousness. These "qualities" don't go away when we become Christians. They come out whenever people get together—even a group of redeemed people in the church!

Paul reminded his friends that God started with some very raw material when he chose them to be his people. "Consider your own call, brothers and sisters: not many of you were wise by human standards, not many were powerful, not many were of noble birth. But God chose what is foolish...God chose what is weak...God chose what is low and despised in the world, things that are not...so that no one may boast in the presence of the Lord" (1 Cor. 1:26-29). The miracle of the church is that God brings together such imperfect people to serve and glorify him. He does not restrict the membership of the Kingdom to the elite of our world. He intentionally calls weak, foolish, and despicable people into his service—so that he can demonstrate his power through them!

"But wait a minute," you may say. "That's the element I see missing here. With all of their quarreling, dissention, and immorality, how is God's power being demonstrated in this church?"

You see exactly the point Paul is driving at: The Corinthians are not yet the people that God intends them to be.

The Shaky "Middle Ground"

The Corinthians are trying to find a kind of "middle ground" where they can live. Their minds are drawn to the things of God, but they aren't yet ready to give up the things of the world. They're trying to live with a foot in heaven and a foot on earth. As a result, their footing is perilously shaky. Romans 7:14-24 describes the turmoil going on in their individual hearts: "I can will what is right, but I cannot do it. For I do not do the good I want, but the evil I do not want is what I do. Now if I do what I do not want, it is no longer I that do it, but sin that dwells within me" (Rom. 7:18b-20).

The Corinthians have not yet moved to the kind of life Paul described in Romans 8. They are not yet "set free from the law of sin and of death" (Rom. 8:2). Paul's whole purpose in writing to the Corinthians—indeed, his purpose in writing to us—is to explain how we can move beyond this "middle ground" to the higher ground of Christian living that God intends for us.

Many people are surprised to learn that Christians remain subject to human passions that run contrary to God's will. They are even more surprised to learn that God can change all that; when they stumble upon this truth, it strikes them as an entirely new idea. It's the idea that Paul unfolds in his First Epistle to the Corinthians.

God Provides A Way

At the end of the first chapter, Paul begins to show us how God has provided a way to measure up to the calling he has given us. He writes, "[God] is the source of your life in Christ Jesus, who became for us wisdom from God, and righteousness and sanctification and redemption, in order that, as it is written, Let the one who boasts, boast in the Lord" (1 Cor. 1:30-31). God calls us to be holy people. He assigns us the task of representing him in the world. He enjoins us to show to the world his own character in everything that we do. The only way we can do all these things, the only way we can be all of these things, is if he enables us. And that's exactly what God does.

Paul says that only God can be the source of our life in Christ Jesus. In our own human logic, we often cannot discern what we should do; so God becomes our wisdom. We are tempted not to live uprightly and cleanly in an immoral world; so God becomes our righteousness. We are assaulted by every sort of spiritual pollution that would corrupt our hearts and minds; so God becomes our sanctification. We are weak in the face of evil and liable to fall under the accusations of our spiritual Enemy; so God becomes our redemption. We can live victoriously day by day, because God continues to win the victory in our lives.

Many well-intentioned theologians have obscured Paul's point with abstract notions of "forensic righteousness" and the like. But the Bible does not lead us off on such tangents. Paul is not describing some sort of mystical substitution that God makes on our behalf. He does not propose a cosmic game of "let's pretend," in which God overlooks the spiritual corruption and frailty that remain in a Christian's life. No, Paul is talking in very practical terms. He is saying that God can change us, spiritually and morally, so that we become holy people. He is saying that a vital part of the redeeming work of Christ is to implant God within our lives, so that God's own qualities of wisdom, righteousness, and holiness become our qualities as well. Consider this word of testimony from Hannah Whitall Smith, a Quaker woman of Philadelphia who discovered the truth of this Scripture text about a century ago:

> ...What had come to me now was a discovery, and in no sense an attainment. I had not become a better woman than I was before, but I had found out that Christ was a better Savior than I had thought He was. I was not one bit more able to conquer my temptations than I had been in the past, but I had

discovered that He was able and willing to conquer them for me. I had no more wisdom or righteousness of my own than I had ever had, but I had found out that He could really and actually be made unto me, as the Apostle declared He would be, wisdom, and righteousness, and sanctification, and redemption.

I shall never forget the first time this declaration was proved to me to be, not only a pious saying, but a downright fact. Shortly after I had come to know something of the fulness of Christ's salvation, an occasion arose in my life when I realized that I should have need of a very large amount of patience. An individual, who was especially antagonistic to me, was coming to spend two weeks at our house. She had always in the past been very provoking and irritating, and I felt, as the day drew near for her arrival, that, if I was to behave to her in a really Christ-like way, I should need a far greater supply of patience than I usually possessed.... Therefore one night, after the rest of the family had retired, I shut myself up in my room, taking with me a plate of biscuits, which I had provided in case I should be hungry; and kneeling down by my bed, I prepared myself for an all-night conflict. I confess I felt rather like a martyr.... But scarcely had my knees touched the floor when, like a flash, there came into my mind the declaration to which I have referred, "But of him are ye in Christ Jesus, who of God is made unto us wisdom, and righteousness, and sanctification, and redemption; that, according as it is written, he that glorieth, let him glory in the Lord." "Yes," I exclaimed inwardly, "and of course patience as well!" And I arose at once from my knees, with an absolute conviction that I did not in the least need, as I had thought, to lay in a big stock of patience to use during my friend's visit, but that I could simply, as the occasion arose, look to the Lord for a present supply for my present need.[1]

Hannah Smith learned to receive from the Lord "a present supply for my present need." That's what Paul challenges us to do. As the Spirit of Christ controls our lives, he lives through us. His characteristics become ours. His sufficiency becomes ours. His holiness becomes ours.

"Know Nothing But Christ—Crucified!"

Paul makes an arresting statement at the beginning of 1 Corinthians 2. In the preceding verses, he has praised the Corinthians for their knowledge and their articulate ability to argue for the Christian faith. But then he says, "I decided to know nothing among you except Jesus Christ, and him crucified" (1 Cor. 2:2). He says that he did not try to use artful words or inexorable logic to win them to the Lord. He simply determined to live like the Lord himself— the crucified Lord.

Like most of the first-century Greek world, the Christians at Corinth were enamored with philosophy. The "golden age" of Greece had left them with a passion for dialogue and argumentation. In every major Greek city, one could still find learned men debating the great issues of life, as Paul found in Athens (Acts 17:16ff.). But Paul does not portray Jesus Christ as being a more sophisticated thinker than the other philosophers of the day. He does not try to demonstrate the magical powers of Jesus, as the cultic miracle workers and sorcerers tried to do. Instead he presents Jesus as One who is humble, servile, and willing to suffer for others—even to die. As Christ's representative, that is how Paul himself lives. He labors "in fear and much trembling" (1 Cor. 2:3), because he knows that he has been called to minister as Christ did.

Notice how different this is from the high-profile Christian ministries of our day. Don't get me wrong. I am grateful that thousands of people have heard the Word of God through radio and television evangelism. Billy Graham and his team are but one notable example of media evangelists who have carried out the Great Commission to reach the world. Several others have been faithful in this ministry as well. But I am troubled by the attitude that so many radio and TV evangelists demonstrate week after week. They display an arrogance that is utterly foreign to the spirit of New Testament Christianity. They demonstrate their love for expensive buildings, flashy clothes, and costly jewels. They exhort their viewers to expect these things from God. Like the Christians at Corinth, they try to camp on a kind of "middle ground" between heaven and earth. The result is that their ministries make a ridiculous parody of the Kingdom of God. I am sure that the heavenly Father is grieved by this.

I believe the Father is pained just as much by ministries that strain to make themselves "respectable" in the eyes of the intellectual crowd. True, God expects us to use our minds for his glory; he gives us wonderful opportunities to learn and to use our knowledge to promote his work. And we have seen some powerful Christian intellects, such as C.S. Lewis, who have given an articulately reasoned defense of the Christian faith in our time. God send us more of them! Yet God save us from the temptation to cloak the gospel message in high-brow sophisticated reasoning, simply to impress a skeptical world. Intellectual persuasion does not beget faith; only the power of God can do that (1 Cor. 2:4-5).

For these reasons, Paul says that you and I are called to model our lives after Christ the Crucified. He was despised and rejected in this world. He was nailed to the cross because the world did not understand him (1 Cor. 2:8). We are called to live like that and, as we shall see in 2 Corinthians, we are called to die like that.

An Example: The Apostles

A good preacher knows how to use practical illustrations that his listeners can readily grasp. Paul is a master at this. So all of chapter 2 is an illustration of the Christ-life that he is challenging us to have. Paul says that if we want to know what he's talking about, there are some examples close at hand. He invites us to start with Paul himself. Then, as the chapter unfolds, he invites us to look at all of the apostles as examples of people who live as Christ lives, with the Spirit of Christ ruling their lives.[2]

He says the apostles "do speak wisdom, though it is not a wisdom of this age or of the rulers of this age, who are doomed to perish" (1 Cor. 2:6). They are being misunderstood by the wise people of their day, just as Jesus was misunderstood. Many of them will be martyred, just as Jesus was martyred.

The pivotal verse of this chapter—indeed, of the entire letter—is 2:12: "Now we [i.e., the apostles] have received not the spirit of the world, but the Spirit that is from God…."

Don't all Christians receive the Holy Spirit when they are saved? Yes. Even before conversion, the Holy Spirit speaks to a person's heart and mind, drawing that person to the Lord (John 6:44; 1 Cor. 12:3; cf. Heb. 12:25). This is what John Wesley called "preventing grace" or prevenient grace.[3] (In Wesley's day, the term "prevent" had the meaning of "precede.") When a person is converted, the Holy Spirit confirms inwardly that a life-giving change has taken place (Rom. 8:15-16; 1 John 5:6-12). And from that moment on, the Holy Spirit begins to change a Christian's life so that anyone can see a transformation is taking place. As Paul tells the Corinthians, "…You are a letter of Christ, prepared by us, written not with ink but with the Spirit of the living God, not on tablets of stone but on tablets of human hearts" (2 Cor. 3:3). So in each of these respects, yes, every Christian has the Holy Spirit.

Likewise the Corinthians had received the Holy Spirit. Yet Paul makes a clear distinction between what the Holy Spirit is doing in the apostles' lives and what he is doing in the strife-torn Corinthians' lives. Notice what he says.

First, he says the apostles have received the Holy Spirit "so that we may understand the gifts bestowed on us by God" (1 Cor. 2:12). By contrast, the Corinthians don't understand the spiritual gifts they have received and are using them inappropriately (chaps. 12-14).

Second, he says the apostles have received the Holy Spirit so they may teach other Christians under the Spirit's direction, to the point that even the words they use are "taught by the Spirit" (1 Cor. 2:13). By contrast, the Corinthians are speaking hatefully to one another and bickering in a most ungodly manner. "For as long as there is jealousy and quarreling among you, are you not of the flesh," Paul asks, "and behaving according to human inclinations?" (1 Cor. 3:3).

Third, he says the apostles have received the Holy Spirit so they can discern what the Lord is doing and act in harmony with him.

He says, "We have the mind of Christ" (1 Cor. 2:16). By contrast, the Corinthians have condoned gross immorality by some of their members. "It is actually reported that there is sexual immorality among you, and of a kind that is not found even among pagans;... And you are arrogant! Should you not rather have mourned, so that he who has done this would have been removed from among you?" (1 Cor. 5:1-2).

How can this be? How can the Corinthians have the Holy Spirit, yet be unspiritual? How can they be saved from sin, yet live sinfully? The answer is simple. They are still "doing what comes naturally"—to their human nature, that is.

Remember what Peter learned about himself as he lived and labored with Jesus? When Peter declared that Jesus was the Messiah, the Lord said, "Blessed are you, Simon son of Jonah! For flesh and blood has not revealed this to you, but my Father in heaven" (Matt. 16:17). The Holy Spirit spoke to Peter's heart and Peter repeated what he heard. But just five verses later, Peter counseled Jesus to avoid the cross. So the Lord said, "Get behind me, Satan! You are a stumbling block to me; for you are setting your mind not on divine things but on human things" (Matt. 16:23). Did this mean that Peter had received the Holy Spirit, then lost him again? No. The problem was that he listened to both the Holy Spirit and the spirit of Satan. So long as he did that, he was a "stumbling block" to the Lord. The same was true of the Corinthians.

The same is true of you and me.

Paul emphasizes in 1 Corinthians 2 that the Holy Spirit was operating in the lives of the apostles in a radically different way than he did in the lives of the Corinthians. The apostles' lives illustrate what the Holy Spirit can do when he is given full rein within someone's life. God desires that every believer live like this. "Do you not know that you are God's temple and that God dwells in you?" Paul asks the Corinthians. "...God's temple is holy, and you are that temple" (1 Cor. 3:16-17). In these verses, he uses the plural word for *you*. He is referring to the entire congregation of believers in Corinth. He challenges everyone in the church to be "saints" or "holy ones" in the world where they live, just as the apostles are. It's clear that many of the Corinthians are not yet equipped to fulfil that calling, but God still calls them to it. That's why Paul is writing to them.

What Happened at Pentecost?

The only way we can understand what made the apostles different is to go back to the Day of Pentecost. Here we pick up the thread of the story begun by the Gospel of Mark.

You'll recall that the second half of Mark's Gospel explored the question of who the disciples were. We saw that they were continually squabbling among themselves and grieving the heart of their Master. As Mark closes, they are in the same predicament as the Corinthians. Mark records that the last time Jesus appeared to them in the flesh, he "upbraided them for their lack of faith and stubbornness" (Mark 16:14). Then he gave them the Great Commission to "go into all the world and proclaim the good news to the whole creation" (Mark 16:15ff.). What an impossible job assignment for faithless, stubborn men!

So Jesus told them not to start their work yet. He told them to wait in Jerusalem until they received the power to do what he had called them to do. "For John baptized with water," he said, "but you will be baptized with the Holy Spirit not many days from now" (Acts 1:5). He was speaking to believers. In fact, he was speaking to believers who had been discipled under his personal tutelage for three years. He told them that they were not yet ready to take up the calling he had given them. "But you will receive power when the Holy Spirit has come upon you," Jesus promised, "and you will be my witnesses in Jerusalem, in all Judea and Samaria, and to the ends of the earth" (Acts 1:8). A.B. Simpson has good insight here:

> …The greatest danger about these men was not in what they might fail to do, but in what they might try to do. The greatest harm that we can do is the attempt to do anything at all when we are not prepared, and when we do not understand our Master's will. Suppose a regiment of soldiers should start off without their captain's orders, or their necessary equip-

ment or artillery; the next attempt of the army would be ren-
dered more hopeless by their rash exposure and needless failure.

And so the Master wants to keep us from doing anything,
until we are prepared to go forth in his strength and victory.
Our hardest lesson to learn is to unlearn, and to know our
utter helplessness....

The deepest experience into which they had to enter was self-
crucifixion, and crucifixion is the death not only of the evil
self, but of the strong and self-sufficient self.[4]

The Christian believers gathered in Jerusalem, waiting and
watching for the change that Christ had promised would occur in
their lives. There were about 120 people in that congregation (Acts
1:15). On the Day of Pentecost, "All of them were filled with the
Holy Spirit and began to speak in other languages, as the Spirit gave
them ability" (Acts 2:4). They immediately began the work of evangelism that Jesus had given them to do.

What made the difference in the apostles? The Holy Spirit, who
filled them with the very nature of Jesus Christ. Skeptics could see
what a radical change had occurred in their lives as a result of the
Spirit's coming.

Double-minded Peter became a firebrand preacher for Jesus
Christ before thousands of Jews, who could have mobbed him and
bludgeoned him to death. Instead, about 3,000 of them accepted
Jesus Christ as their Savior that day (Acts 2:41).

The same men who told Jesus to send the crowds away because
they didn't have enough bread for them all (Mark 6:35ff.) now
invited the 3,000 converts to share "the apostles' teaching and fellowship,... the breaking of bread and the prayers" (Acts 2:42). "Day
by day...they broke bread at home and ate their food with glad and
generous hearts, praising God and having the goodwill of all the
people" (vv. 46-47).

The same men who scratched their heads in puzzlement when
they could not help a demoniac boy are now inviting cripples to
stand and walk (Acts 3:1ff.). "A great number of people would also
gather from the towns around Jerusalem, bringing the sick and

those tormented by unclean spirits, and they were all cured" (Acts 5:16).

The Holy Spirit had given them power, not for show, but for service. He had swept away their all-too-human selfishness and replaced it with Jesus' own compassion for suffering people. The Day of Pentecost was thus an historical milestone for the Christian Church.

Yet after Pentecost, we seldom see the Holy Spirit transforming peoples' lives in this manner at the moment of their conversion. The Book of Acts and Paul's letters illustrate repeatedly that most Christians are not "filled" with the Holy Spirit or "baptized" by the Holy Spirit until some time after they are converted. What accounts for this?

The Order of Redemption

John Wesley was a brilliant theologian with a knack for describing the spiritual life in simple English. He learned from his study of Scripture and his observation of everyday life that a person moves through several stages of growth as God deals with his soul. He called this "the order of redemption."

First, Wesley said, a person who lives in an unregenerate state is a sinner. But even such a person feels the tug of the Holy Spirit in his heart. "No man living is entirely destitute of what is vulgarly called *natural conscience*," Wesley wrote. "But this is not natural: it is more properly termed *preventing grace*. Every man has a greater or less measure of this, which waiteth not for the call of man. Every man has, sooner or later, good desires, although the generality of men stifle them before they can strike deep root, or produce any considerable fruit."[5]

As God speaks to a person's heart through this "preventing grace," that person may repent of his sin. He may ask God's forgiveness. If so, God promises to pardon that sinner and give him an inward sense that he has been forgiven. The Bible (and Wesley) call this event *justification*.

Simultaneous with this is the "new birth." As Wesley says, justification refers to the "great work which God does *for us*, in forgiving our sins; the latter [new birth], to the great work which God does *in us*, in renewing our fallen nature."[6] God gives us a desire to seek his will and serve him. We make a fresh beginning in life, starting the walk of faith with him. Theologians also call this *regeneration*.

God accomplishes a tremendous change in a person's life through the regeneration, but he does not intend to stop there. I'm afraid this fact is widely misunderstood. The bulk of our evangelical preaching implies that a person must make a decision to live for Christ, period. It leaves people with the notion that a Christian must deal with the struggles and failures of spiritual immaturity as long as he lives on this earth. But First Corinthians contradicts that idea. The whole New Testament contradicts it. The "new birth" is just the beginning of a spiritual growth process that lasts for a lifetime.

Wesley called the next phase of this process *sanctification*, though he also used the terms "holiness," "Christian perfection," and being "strong in the Lord." He referred to a higher plane of spiritual growth, where the Holy Spirit sets us free from "evil thoughts and evil tempers." Sooner or later, Wesley says, every Christian realizes the need for further growth.

> …It is properly a conviction, wrought by the Holy Ghost, of the *sin* which still *remains* in our heart; of the *phronēma sarkos, the carnal mind*, which "does still remain (as our church speaks), even in them that are regenerate"; although it does no longer *reign*; it has not now dominion over them. It is a conviction of our proneness to evil, of a heart bent to backsliding, of the still continuing tendency of the flesh to lust against the Spirit. Sometimes, unless we continually watch and pray, it lusteth to pride, sometimes to anger, sometimes to love of the world, love of ease, love of honour, or love of pleasure more than of God. It is a conviction of the tendency of our heart to self will, to atheism or idolatry, and, above all, to unbelief, whereby, in a thousand ways, and under a thousand pre-

tenses, we are ever departing, more or less, from the living God.

> …Where we least suspected it, we find a taint of pride or self will, of unbelief or idolatry; so that we are now more ashamed of our best duties than formerly of our worst sins: and hence we cannot but feel, that these are so far from having any-thing meritorious in them, yea, so far from being able to stand in sight of the divine justice, that for those also we should be guilty before God, were it not for the blood of the covenant.[7]

I think that's a telling line: "We are now more ashamed of our best duties than formerly of our worst sins." Only after a Christian has begun to grow in sensitivity to the Spirit of God can he realize his need for God's indwelling power. Only then can he feel the pitiful futility of any good thing he might do to merit the favor of God.

There's nothing defective with our conversion experience, but conversion only starts us on the path of further insight into the real nature of our relationship with God. As we mature in the Christian life, we realize more keenly our dependence on God for everything that we do. We realize that nothing redemptive can come from our own efforts; it must be all of God, or it can be nothing. When we grasp this fact, we yield ourselves completely to the Holy Spirit, allowing him to accomplish in us the work that only he can do.

How Do We Receive Him?

Paul challenges the Corinthians—indeed, he challenges us—to move beyond self-serving, carnal attitudes to receive the fullness of Christ's Spirit within us. He calls us to be sanctified for God's ser-vice. How can we do this?

First, Paul says, we need to realize that we receive every good thing from God. "What do you have that you did not receive? And if you received it, why do you boast as if it were not a gift?" (1 Cor. 4:7). Every spiritual gift is exactly that—a gift. God saved us from the penalty of sin. He gave us the new birth. He offers us the free-dom from ungodly motives and desires. We cannot attain, earn, or merit any of these things; they are grace-gifts from the heavenly Father.

Second, Paul says, we must embrace our calling to live like Christ in this world. He again contrasts the apostles' way of life with that of the Christians at Corinth. "We are fools for the sake of Christ," he says, while the Corinthians are trying to be "wise in Christ" (1 Cor. 4:10). "We are weak," while the Corinthians profess to be "strong" (v. 10). The Corinthians maneuver for positions of respectability and honor, while the apostles are content to live "in disrepute" (v. 10). "We are hungry and thirsty, we are poorly clothed and beaten and homeless, and we grow weary from the work of our own hands. When reviled, we bless; when persecuted, we endure; when slandered, we speak kindly" (vv. 11-13). The Corinthians certainly would not respond in this way, would they? So he admonishes them, "Be imitators of me, as I am of Christ" (11:1; cf. 4:16). If we truly want the Spirit of Christ to live within us, we must be ready to live as Christ lives.

Third, Paul says, we must "come to a sober and right mind, and sin no more" (1 Cor. 15:34). Paul will not allow the Corinthians to rationalize their incest, debauchery, or other forms of sin. He makes it emphatically clear that Christians do not indulge in sin. Anyone who thinks he can be a Christian and continue to sin is not in his "right mind."

Finally, Paul says, we must be ready to die. He echoes the words of Jesus when he says, "Fool! What you sow does not come to life unless it dies" (1 Cor. 15:36). He is speaking primarily of physical death. The Greek thinkers of his day devised all sorts of theories to grapple with the painful reality of death. Since the Corinthians were anxious not to appear foolish to their friends, I imagine they "bought into" some of these theories. But Paul says a Christian needn't be afraid of physical death. It is the gateway to eternal life with Christ.

I see something more here, though. I believe Paul is implying that the only real fool is the person who tries to preserve himself, instead of entrusting himself to Christ. If we want to live like Christ, we literally must be ready to die, because the world's need for sacrificial love did not end at Calvary. E. Stanley Jones writes:

> A visiting and very pompous bishop asked some village people in India who were candidates for baptism, "What is it to be a Christian?" and expected a theological reply, but got this answer instead, "To live like Mr. Murray." Mr. Murray was the missionary who had taught them. The word of Christianity had become flesh in him. It was so in Jesus.[8]

Martyrdom is the privilege of every Christian, because the only way that Jesus Christ can live in our world is for you and me to die. Some died in the Colosseum; some died in the Nazi prisons; while some are dying in the factories, offices, and a thousand other places where humble service is needed. Believe me, the death of a self-willed ego can be just as painful as the death of one's physical body. But when the ego dies and Christ begins to live through us, the world is transformed. The Holy Spirit does that when we're ready to move on to the "higher ground."

Endnotes

[1] Hannah Whitall Smith, *The Unselfishness of God* (Princeton, N.J.: Littlebrook Publishing, 1987) pp. 193-194.

[2] It's very important to note the transition that occurs in 1 Cor. 2:1, where Paul says, "When I came to you, brothers and sisters, I did not come proclaiming the mystery of God to you in lofty words or wisdom." The "I" in this passage refers to Paul himself. Consequently, the word "we" in this chapter refers to others who came to Corinth proclaiming the gospel—-i.e., the apostles. Clearly, chapter 2 does not use "we" to refer to all Christians, because Paul sets the Spirit-controlled life that "we" experience in stark contrast to the life of the Corinthians in chapter 3.

[3] Thomas Jackson, ed., *The Works of Reverend John Wesley*, third ed. (London: John Mason, 1829), vol. VI:509.

[4] A.B. Simpson, *The Holy Spirit, or, Power from on High, Vol. II* (Harrisburg, Pa.: Christian Publications, n.d.), pp. 69-70.

[5] Jackson, vol. VI:512.

[6] N. Burwash, ed., *Wesley's 52 Standard Sermons* (Salem, Ohio: Schmul Publishing Company, 1967), p. 447.

[7] Burwash, pp. 432-433.

[8] E. Stanley Jones, *The Way* (Nashville, Tenn.: Abingdon- Cokesbury, 1946), p. 290.

7

"Look Not To Your Own Interests"

Philippians 2:5-11 is the best-known passage of Scripture concerning the mind of Christ. Some modern translations render it in such a way that the word *mind* is not used; but Paul employs the same Greek verb that occurs in Mark 8, where Jesus tells Peter he does not think as God thinks. The Greek word *(phroneite)* literally means "to be minded"—in this case, to be minded as God is minded:

> Let each of you look not to your own interests, but to the interests of others. Let the same mind be in you that was in Christ Jesus, who, though he was in the form of God, did not regard equality with God as something to be exploited, but emptied himself, taking the form of a slave, being born in human likeness (vv. 5-7).

Most scholars deal with verses 5-11 as if they were a unit, an ancient Christian hymn to the Christ. Perhaps they were. But I believe Paul used these words to illustrate the message he wished to convey to the Philippians.

A state of conflict existed within the Philippian church, and Paul wrote out of his desire to see that conflict resolved. Any time people work together, tensions will develop. But unresolved tension brings reproach on the cause of Christ. Paul knew that this conflict could be resolved only if the Philippians had a change of heart—and a change of mind.

In chapter 1, Paul observes that some people preach Christ out of right motives, while others preach Christ out of contentiousness: "Some proclaim Christ from envy and rivalry, but others from goodwill. These proclaim Christ out of love, knowing that I have been put here for the defense of the gospel; the others proclaim Christ out of selfish ambition…" (1:15-17a). Here Paul uses the Greek word *eritheia*, which literally means "to strive." Paul condemns the tendency to contend for one's own way, which is at the heart of carnal thinking.

He introduces the second chapter with these words: "If then there is any encouragement in Christ, any consolation from love, any sharing in the Spirit, any compassion and sympathy, make my joy complete: be of the same mind, having the same love, being in full accord and of one mind" (2:1-2). The basic problem at Philippi was that the Christians had different "minds"; each one thought his own way. So if Paul was to heal their division, he had to deal with the mind. He describes the sort of mind they must have:

> Do nothing from selfish ambition (Gk., *eritheia*) or conceit, but in humility regard others as better than yourselves. Let each of you look not to your own interests, but to the interest of others (2:3-4).

The first time I read that in the Greek, I thought, *Wait a minute. Where is the word "only"?* The King James Version put the word *only* in italics, which indicates it is not in the original Greek text. Try as I might, I couldn't find it in the Greek. So I went to our classical Greek specialist at the college, who has a Ph.D.. in classical languages from St. Louis University, and I said, "Help me here." He cast about for awhile and then wrote me a note that said: "It isn't there, Kinlaw."

I went to Bob Mulholland, who has a Ph.D.. from Harvard in New Testament. I said, "Bob, I've got a question…." He pulled books down and looked all around his office. Finally, he said, "Kinlaw, it isn't there."

Now why is the word *only* inserted in that verse, in most modern translations of the Bible? Why do most versions read, "Let each of you look not *only* to your own interests, but *also* to the interests of others"? Because we twentieth-century Christians don't believe the Lord can deliver us from self-interest, so we insert our assumptions into Scripture.

Four Ungodly Characteristics

In verses 3 and 14, Paul lists four characteristics that should be alien to the Christian life. He says that every Christian should act (1) without self-interest; (2) without vain conceit; (3) without grumbling; and (4) without questioning.

Self-interest (v. 3) is the supreme characteristic of a sinful person. It has been said that sinfulness is to be "curved inward upon oneself." Conversely, the purpose of the redemption offered by Christ is to undo our distorted orientation—to turn us outward, so that we are not interested in ourselves but in the well-being of others. When we understand sin in these terms, we begin to break down the traditional dichotomy between evangelism and Christian social action. After all, the Christian life is not an "either/or" proposition: "Either I enrich my own relationship with Christ, or I go out and show others who Christ is, through my selfless service." Outwardness is all there is to the gospel. The essence of Christian living is making oneself a servant as Christ is a servant.

It is no accident that John Wesley became a paragon of Christian social action. He engaged in prison reform, slave emancipation, hospital work, and other activities that modern evangelicals sometimes disparage as the concerns of "the social gospel" (as if it were different from the gospel of Christ). These activities were a normal consequence of Wesley's message about the necessity of entering into the Christ-life.

Self-interest is well demonstrated by the question, "What's in it for me?" Jesus never strived to get something for himself. The

Gospels relate no instance in which Jesus' self-interest was his first consideration.[1]

Imagine the scene when Jairus asked Jesus to heal his daughter. Suppose Jesus had said, "Yes, I could do that. I could go home with you and lay my hands on your daughter, and she would get well. *But what's in it for me?*" My mentioning such an idea must offend you, because that attitude is utterly antithetical to what Jesus represented. He came to lay down his life for his sheep (John 10:15). He did not come to protect himself; rather, he came to spend himself.

The Old Testament lifestyle may have been expressed by the statement, "Love your neighbor as yourself" (Lev. 19:18). But Jesus expressed the New Testament lifestyle like this: "Love one another as I have loved you. No one has greater love than this, to lay down one's life for one's friends" (John 15:12-13). Jesus changed the pattern of personal priorities when he became the Shepherd who sacrificed himself for his sheep.

Conceit (v. 3) is the common English translation of the New Testament Greek term *kenodoxía*, which comes from the word *kenos*, meaning "empty." In other words, a Christian should be unconcerned about elevating his own status or doing things for the sake of appearance.

How often we fall short of doing God's will because we are overly concerned about appearance! I have noticed that at an annual conference of ministers, when someone asks, "What can you tell me about your church?" a fellow will quail or strut, depending on the position of his congregation in the "pecking order." I don't think I have ever heard a minister say, "I have the appointment of my life. There are dozens of people in that community who don't know Christ, and I have an opportunity to reach them." We think instead of our status and position.

Jesus exemplified a life unconcerned with appearance. He talked with a Samaritan woman; he touched lepers; he cared nothing about his appearances before his disciples or the public.

Murmuring (v. 14) is the self-pitying attitude that says, "I deserve better than this." Self-pity is another mark of our fallenness.

When Helen Roseveare graduated from Cambridge in the early 1960s, she went to an area of Zaire where two hundred thousand people lived without a doctor. She made that her mission field. As her medical work progressed, she decided to build a hospital. She wrote her mother, asking for a book about how to build a hospital; her mother was unable to find such a book, but sent her a book about how to make bricks. So Helen Roseveare found herself teaching the African natives how to make kiln-fired bricks.

As they were taking the first load from the kiln, and she began pulling the spines off of the new bricks, she realized that her fingers were wet. They were dripping blood where she had broken her fingernails. She thought, *Lord, I didn't come to Africa to make brick; I came here to be a surgeon. Surely there's someone in England who could come to do this.*

While she stood there feeling sorry for herself, a runner came from the hospital and said, "We have an emergency. Come! You must perform surgery immediately!"

She went to the infirmary and began to prepare for surgery. She gritted her teeth as she scrubbed her hands with a brush; then she let her assistant pour alcohol over them, and her protest became a scream.

A few weeks later, one of the African workers at the kiln said, "Doctor, when you are in the surgery you are like a god. You terrify us. But when you're at the brick kiln and your fingers drip blood like ours, you're our sister. We love you!" At that moment, she realized God had not sent her to Africa to be a surgeon; he had sent her there to show the love of Christ. What did she deserve? Merely an opportunity to show the love of Christ. And she could not do that if she got what she thought she deserved!

Arguing (v. 14) is the mentality that tries to bargain with God. It is the attitude that says, "Yes, Lord, but…." Or, "Isn't there a better way to do this, Lord?" It professes a willingness to obey, but it hedges.

Arguing is the attitude of a Christian girl who marries a fellow that she knows is not really God's choice. It is the attitude of a young man who is called to serve God overseas, but allows himself to get trapped by career or family obligations at home. Arguing rears its head in a thousand ways, as we compromise the will of God in our lives by placing conditions upon it.

Future Hope or Present Reality?

Can you imagine a person who is not characterized by self-interest? A person who is not a slave to appearances? A person who is not always feeling he deserves better? Or a person who does not answer God's will with conditions? That would be the sort of person God could use! That person would be a part of the answer, rather than a part of the problem of evangelizing the world.

The Philippians and Corinthians had made themselves part of the problem. So Paul exhorted them to have the same mind which was in Christ. Christ had the attitude of a humble, obedient servant—the opposite of one who strives to protect his own interests. On the night before the cross, he said, "Father, glorify your Son." How was he glorified? By the cross, not by the crown. Christians are to find their glory in the same way, by renouncing all that serves self and by pouring out their lives for others.

Is that sheer idealism? Is it a goal toward which many people strive, but which no one attains? Is it to be accomplished in another world? In another world, such a life would be far less valuable than it is here. In the new world where Christ will reign, everyone will be like that! But this world needs to see the grace of Christ now; the unsaved masses long to see people who can live like that right now.

Jesus said, "Whoever listens to you listens to me, and whoever rejects you rejects me, and whoever rejects me rejects the one who sent me" (Luke 10:16). Christians are Christ to the world. This is what Paul meant when he said, "...To me, living is Christ" (Phil. 1:21). We usually interpret that verse to mean that Christ gave significance to his life. But it also means that Paul's life gave Christ significance to other people. The only way the world will know Christ is through us. Therefore, there must be a correspondence between our lives and the life of the One we represent. Otherwise the world will never know who he is.

One tragic night, Helen Roseveare was raped by a band of rebel soldiers. Amid the anguish and agony of that dark night, she wondered, *How can God let this happen to me?* Immediately, she sensed the Lord saying to her, "Thank you, Helen. Thank you for letting me use your body. They are not raping you; they are raping me."

Afterwards she was locked up with a Roman Catholic nun who had also been raped. The nun was emotionally shattered because her vow of chastity had been broken. Helen tried to comfort her. "You did not sin," Helen said. "Remember the Virgin Mary. Everyone in the community thought she was an adulteress because she was unmarried and pregnant."

The nun gasped in horror. "How could anyone call Mary an adulteress?" she asked.

"That is what the people in Nazareth thought," Helen continued. "Yet she was pure, and you are just as pure. And think of this: The fact that you were raped may have saved someone else from being raped." She shared with the nun what she had heard from the Lord: *They are not raping you; they are raping me.*

Christ has no way to take the wrath of the world upon himself, except through us. When people of the world heap ridicule and persecution upon us, they heap it upon him. His life must be seen in this world, not only in the next world.

Is it possible for any human being to be Christ in the present world? Philippians 2 says it is. Paul never says that there are a great many people like this; but he does say there are some. Paul himself is one. Timothy is another. In fact, Paul says Timothy's other-oriented life proves his fitness for Christian ministry: "I hope in the Lord Jesus to send Timothy to you soon.... I have no one like him who will be genuinely concerned for your welfare. All of them are seeking their own interests, not those of Jesus Christ" (Phil. 2:19-21).

The Philippians and Corinthians could also become examples of other-oriented living. How? Not by striving for it. Not by imitating

Christ or emulating him. Notice how Paul says this can happen: "Therefore, my beloved, just as you have always obeyed me, not only in my presence, but much more now in my absence, work out your own salvation with fear and trembling; *for God is at work in you, enabling you both to will and to work for his good pleasure*" (Phil. 2:12-13, italics added). God has no pleasure in our self-interest; but he has great pleasure in our sacrificing ourselves for his sake. God has no pleasure in our proper appearances; but he does take pleasure in our humbling ourselves to serve him. God has no pleasure in our murmuring, for that denies his sovereignty and his goodness; but he takes great pleasure in our being content with the situation in which he has placed us. God has no pleasure in our arguing, for that obstructs our faithfulness to him; but he takes great pleasure in our obedience, even when obedience leads to death.

How We Can Have the Mind of Christ

Becoming like Christ is a work of grace. It occurs only as Christ lives within us, not as we strive to be like him. Is this possible? Of course it is! Christian history is brimming with examples of men and women who have responded to life as Christ responded. They did it because Christ lived within them.

During Samuel Brengle's senior year at Boston University, he was offered the pastorate of a wealthy congregation in South Bend, Indiana. He had an opportunity to begin his ministry at the top of the social roster. But he felt that God was calling him to join the Salvation Army, so he crossed the Atlantic and presented himself to General William Booth.

"We don't want you. You're dangerous," Booth said.

"Dangerous? What do you mean?" Brengle asked.

"You would not take orders."

"But you haven't given me a trial," Brengle pleaded.

"You have too much education. You would not be willing to subordinate yourself to one of the officers here. Converted drunks and prostitutes are the staff leaders."

"Please give me a chance," Brengle said. So General Booth sent him to one of his sons, Ballington Booth, who put him through a similar interrogation. When Brengle still insisted on trying the Army, Booth's son made him bootblack for the Central Salvation Army Corps in London. In an unfinished basement, on a dirt floor half-submerged in water, Brengle began cleaning mud off of the boots of converted street bums who were now soldiers in the Army. One day he seemed to hear a voice that said, "You're a fool!"

I am not! he thought.

"You're a sinner, too."

What do you mean?

"Remember the man who buried his talent in the earth?" the inner voice said. "What are you doing here? Think of all the training you've gotten. You're just throwing it away."

Brengle sank into a depression. After awhile he prayed, "Lord, have I failed you? Did I miss your leading?"

And the Lord replied, "Remember, Sam, I washed their feet!"

That muddy cellar became an anteroom to heaven, as Brengle sensed the reassuring presence of his Lord. From that day forward, Brengle knew that he was called, not to invest himself, but to spend himself for others. He realized that Christ is a servant who looks for others to serve with him.

The Holy Spirit makes this sacrificial thinking possible. Jesus' ministry began when the Holy Spirit descended upon him. His disciples' ministry began when the Holy Spirit came upon them at the day of Pentecost, empowering them to "turn the world upside down." Likewise, the Spirit of Christ must control us if we are to be conformed to the character of Christ and filled with his power.

Christ must be free to spend us. As long as we attempt to save our own lives, we shall lose them; but if we surrender our lives to be controlled by his Spirit, we shall live and bear fruit for him. The Bible says very little about self-enrichment; but it says a great deal about giving our lives for the enrichment of others.

Letting Go of the Strings

I recently got acquainted with Josef Tson, the pastor of a large Baptist church in western Romania. Until a few years ago, the Romanian Communist Party was one of the most brutal in the world. As a Christian pastor, Josef spoke out on some issues and angered the government. So they decided to destroy him. They came in and stripped his library of all his books. Two books were quite worn and had no jackets on them, so the soldiers left them behind. One was Martin Niemoller's account of his suffering under Adolf Hitler. The other was *Abundant Living*, a devotional book by E. Stanley Jones.

This Romanian pastor put Martin Niemoller's book on his night stand to give him strength through the night. He put E. Stanley Jones' book on the shelf in his study.

The government then sent the police to interrogate Josef five days a week, and up to seven hours a day. The intent was to destroy him. Oftentimes they would interrogate him with a loaded pistol on the table in front of the interrogator. One day, after a very grueling period of questioning, Josef went into the study, locked the door, and fell to the floor, sobbing. He said, "God, I can't take any more."

He thought he heard a voice. The voice said, "Josef, get up. Read the book on the shelf."

Josef said there was no problem knowing which book to read; there was only one left! So he pulled down E. Stanley Jones' book and opened it. The devotional for that day was on "How to Live Above Your Circumstances." It was about Jesus' facing the cross. Stanley Jones said Jesus did not resist the cross. Jones said that Jesus embraced the cross instead of resisting it.

Josef said, "God, you surely don't mean I'm supposed to embrace my interrogators!"

"Yes," the Lord said, "that's exactly what I mean."

"Well, God, if you want me to do that, you must do something in my heart that you have never done before."

Josef said that's exactly what the Lord did. He walked back into the interrogation room, ready to embrace his trial. He said the change in the atmosphere was almost comical. Before that time, the pastor had been in trauma; but now the chief interrogator was in trauma because he had lost control of his subject! The chief interrogator was beside himself. He finally spun in anger on the pastor and said, "You are stupid. I guess we'll just have to go ahead and kill you."

Josef found himself saying, "I understand, sir. That's your ultimate weapon. When everything else has failed, you can always kill. But you know, I have an ultimate weapon too. And when you use your ultimate weapon, I get to use mine."

"And what's your 'ultimate weapon?'" the Communist angrily demanded.

"Your ultimate weapon is to kill," Josef said. "Mine is to die. When I die, I will be much better off. But your troubles will just be beginning. You see, every tape of every sermon that I have ever preached will be sprinkled with my blood. So you'll have much more trouble with me dead than you have with me alive!"

The Communist shouted, "Take him out!"

A few weeks later, the pastor heard through the grapevine that the Communists were saying Josef Tson was crazy because he wanted to be a martyr. "But we're no fools!" the Communists said. So they stopped interrogating him. Josef said he could not even argue them into killing him then.

"When I was pulling every string to try to save my life, I was at my wit's end," Josef told me. "But when I turned the strings loose and let Christ control my life completely, I was free."

Endnotes

[1]Some may interpret Jesus' practice of withdrawing from the crowds to pray as an act of self-interest, but I doubt that. He seemed to be seeking additional spiritual resources so that he could give of himself to the people.

8

Why We Need the Mind of Christ

Can one person make a difference in the world? Our world is an awfully big place and most of us are remarkably small people; but somewhere deep in the spirit of every human being is the feeling that *my life ought to count for something.* Consciously or unconsciously, every one of us deals sometime with the question, *Can I really make a difference?*

We might eventually convince ourselves that one person could make a difference for another person; but the astounding thing is that the Bible says one person can make a difference to God! We can scarcely believe that we could make a difference to the omnipotent One, yet the Scriptures indicate this is true. At least five passages in the Old Testament suggest it.

First, consider Jeremiah 5:1. God says to Jeremiah, "Go to and fro through the streets of Jerusalem, look around and take note! Search its squares and see if you can find one person who acts justly and seeks truth—so that I may pardon Jerusalem." God says that if the prophet can find a righteous person in the city of Jerusalem, he will forgive the whole city. Jeremiah is unable to find one.

Ezekiel 22 has a similar passage. That entire chapter is quite disturbing. It describes the political leaders of Ezekiel's day as wolves, devouring their own people. Then God describes the religious leaders. He says the priests can no longer tell the difference between the sacred and the profane; they sanctify the profane and profane the holy. He says the prophets claim they have a word from God, but God hasn't given them a word; the word they claim to have from him is a lie. Moreover, God says the ordinary people in the city are preying upon those around them. It's one of the most dismal pictures anywhere in Scripture, even though God is talking about the very City of God. Then in verse 30, he says, "And I sought for anyone among them who would repair the wall and stand in the breach before me on behalf of the land, so that I would not destroy it; but I found no one." God looks for a way to save that sinful city. God says if he can find just one redemptive person, the circumstances will be changed. But he doesn't. So Jerusalem falls.

Here we have an intriguing bit of theology. Did you ever suppose that Omnipotence would have to consider his circumstances? God is the all-powerful One; but in the hour of crisis, he often looks for one person to change his circumstances, so that he can act redemptively.

You see, God has put in our hands the power to resist him. Now he will not strip it away from us. But that very power, if it is turned around, can change God's circumstances. Three passages from Isaiah powerfully illustrate this. The first is found in Isaiah 50: "Why was no one there when I came? Why did no one answer when I called? Is my hand shortened, that it cannot redeem? Or have I no power to deliver? (Isa. 50:2).

God says, "There's nothing wrong with my power. No one has me clamped in an arm lock. I am fully able to save your city. But my power is limited by you yourselves. Because of your own sins, you will be sold into slavery."

Isaiah 59 reveals that God himself has to intervene to punish the injustice he sees. He will not stand idly on the sidelines while innocent people are tortured and killed. "Now the Lord saw, and it was displeasing in His sight that there was no justice. And He saw that there was no man, and was astonished that there was no one to intercede; then His own arm brought salvation to Him; and His righteousness upheld Him" (Isa. 59:15b-16, NASB). Again, the implication is that God will withhold his condemnation of Israel if he can find someone—anyone—to clean up the corruption of his people. But he cannot.

Isaiah 59 also describes the city of Jerusalem and the nation of Israel in the most gruesome terms. Truth has perished in the streets. Justice is not to be found anywhere. The moral darkness is so great that a man stumbles in the middle of the day. The moral darkness is so thick that the people must grope for a wall to guide them home. The moral darkness is so oppressive that they must light their lamps at noon. Surely, God can find someone who's had enough of this to stand up and become a voice for truth and holiness. Just one courageous person can change the course of history for this doomed city. Yet God does not find such a person.

Called to Intervene

Our initial question was, "Can one person make a difference?" Obviously, one person can. But what kind of person? When I found this passage in Isaiah 59, I thought, *Ah! Maybe this is the kind of person who can change God's circumstances. It is someone who's willing to intervene between God and sinful people. God is looking for an intercessor.*

I used to teach Hebrew, so when I get into a fascinating Old Testament passage like this, I like to pull down my Hebrew Bible and see what it says in the Hebrew text. So I wondered what the Hebrew word for *intercede* could teach me. I found it is a very simple word picture, but a very captivating one. The word comes from the Hebrew verb *paga*, which means "to meet" and it is in a grammatical form which means "to cause to meet." It is a participle, so it literally means "a person who causes two other persons to meet." So I thought, *The picture is rather clear: On one hand, you've got a world in its sin and its need; on the other hand, you've got a God who has within himself everything that is necessary to redeem that world. So God is looking for somebody who can bring the Redeemer God and the sinful world together.*

While I was looking up that word in my Hebrew dictionary, I noticed that this particular expression is found only six or seven times in the Old Testament. Two of those are in Isaiah 53. One is the familiar messianic prophecy of Jesus: "…He poured out himself to death, and was numbered with the transgressors; yet he bore the sin of many, and *made intercession* for the transgressors" (Isa. 53:12b, italics added). Here the verb form literally means that Jesus caused the transgressors (i.e., offenders or sinners) to meet with God.

The other usage in Isaiah 53 is found in verse 6: "All we like sheep have gone astray; we have all turned to our own way…." Then my English version does not translate the Hebrew for the rest of that verse very literally, because it says, "…and the Lord has laid on him the iniquity of us all." But here is the same verb that means "to cause to meet," so the Hebrew text literally says, "And the Lord *has caused to meet in him* the iniquities of us all." God was looking for somebody who could bring together the redemptive power of God himself and the sin of the world, someone who could take the two into himself and let them meet, so that our sin could be overcome. That person would be Jesus Christ.

With that, I went back to the passage in Isaiah 59 and noticed something very significant at the end of the sixteenth verse. God said, "I looked for someone who could cause my grace and the world's sin to meet, and I could not find one. So when I could not find one, my own arm brought me salvation" (paraphrase). Until that moment, I had misunderstood what Isaiah means by "the arm of the Lord." I had always imagined the mythical god Jupiter, standing on top of Mount Olympus with lightning bolts in his hand. But because I had just finished reading Isaiah 53, I remembered how that chapter described "the arm of the Lord."

What is the arm of the Lord like? Isaiah 53 says, "He grew up before him like a young plant, and like a root out of dry ground; he had no form or majesty that we should look at him, nothing in his appearance that we should desire him" (Isa. 53:2). The arm of the

Lord was "despised and rejected by others" (v. 3a). The arm of the Lord was "a man of suffering and acquainted with infirmity" (v. 3b). Other people "hid their faces" from the arm of the Lord (v. 3b), not because they feared his power, but because they were embarrassed to see his suffering. People considered the arm of the Lord to be "of no account" (v. 3c). The arm of the Lord took our diseases and our sorrows upon himself (v. 4). The arm of the Lord was pierced for our transgressions and crushed for our iniquities (v. 5a). The punishment that ought to have been ours fell upon the arm of the Lord (v. 5b).

The arm of the Lord is the crucified Jesus. So far as the world can tell, Jesus was an abject failure. But that is the beauty of the power of God. What we call "power," God does not call "power." What we call "weakness" is what God calls "power." So when God could not find a vulnerable person to make things right, he said, "I will have to become that person." When he could not find an intercessor for his people, he began his journey through Bethlehem to the hill called Golgotha.

Salvation never takes place in heaven; salvation can only take place where the problem is. A doctor can't heal a patient in the hospital if the doctor stays at home; the patient in the hospital needs to be touched by capable hands. Likewise, God had to become one of us and take into himself our sin and our evil, in order that we might be redeemed. In the broken, bleeding body of our Lord himself, God's redemptive power and our iniquity came together.

The Lion of the Tribe of Judah

Isaiah says that our God is not redemptive by power; he is redemptive by self-sacrifice. This truth is also shown in the Book of Revelation in a very beautiful way.

Let me take you back to Revelation 4–5. You will remember that the door of heaven has opened and John has looked in to see the throne of God. The twenty-four elders are casting their crowns before him and the living creatures there are crying out, "You are worthy, our Lord and God, to receive glory and honor and power…"

(Rev. 4:11). The One who sits on the throne has in his hand a scroll closed with seven seals. John realizes that in that scroll is his future. In that scroll is your future and mine. So an angel asks, "Who is worthy to open the scroll and break its seals?" (Rev. 5:2). They find nobody in heaven, nobody on earth, nobody under the earth who is worthy to open it. John begins to weep apostolic tears.

Then one of the heavenly creatures says, "Don't waste your tears. There is One worthy to open the book. It is the Lion of the tribe of Judah" (Rev. 5:5, paraphrased).

The Lion of the tribe of Judah was the symbol of David's dynasty. It is a rampant lion, standing on his hind legs with his forelegs extended and his claws out. So when the heavenly messenger says that the Lion of the tribe of Judah is worthy to unroll the future, he indicates that the Deliverer comes from the royal line of King David. John turns to see the Lion of the tribe of Judah. But to his shock, what he sees is not a Lion; it is a Lamb. I think it is significant that in the Book of Revelation, the figure of the Lion appears only one time; but the symbol of the Lamb appears twenty-seven to thirty times (depending on which Greek text you are using). The Book of Revelation repeatedly emphasizes that the Lamb will reign in the new creation that God establishes. He is the Lamb who has been slain from the foundation of the world (Rev. 13:8; cf. Heb. 4:3, Luke 11:49-51).

When I read that passage in Revelation, I remember an experience shared by my Romanian Christian friend, Josef Tson, whom I introduced in an earlier chapter. As you know, one of the most cruel Communist dictatorships in the world was in Romania. A young Romanian Christian could not study for the ministry; no theological seminary was permitted to operate there, because the government was determined to wipe out the church. As a result, the Baptist denomination did not have a single pastor with a good theological education. The Baptist church leaders knew they needed someone with training in theology and church history, so they picked one of their younger men and asked if he would go to the West to get theological training, then come back to lead them.

Josef was that man. He knew that he would pay a heavy price to do this. He could not take his wife and family, and he knew that the government would harass them after he left. If he came back to Romania, he too would be harassed. But for Christ's sake, he felt he should go. So he went to England and completed his theological training.

When he was ready to go back to his homeland, the student Christian group at Cambridge University met together and asked him to share his burden for the future. He told them quite candidly what his prospects were when he went back to Romania. When he finished speaking, a young British student stood up and asked a question. "Josef, this is all very noble of you, willing to go back and expose yourself to persecution," he said. "But what are your chances of success?"

Josef said that when he heard this question, he froze. Here was a markedly Western question. "Success" was not their problem in Romania. Faithfulness was their need. So he thought, *How can I answer this young man without appearing to ridicule him?*

He found himself saying, "What chance of success do I have? I suppose about the same chance of success that a lamb would have, if he were surrounded by a pack of ravening wolves. But if the purpose of the lamb is to reveal to the wolves the nature of what it means to be a lamb, perhaps the best way he can do that is just to let the wolves eat him!"

Suddenly, I got a completely new understanding of the role of Jesus. He came to let a sinful world know what God is like. He knew the hostility in our hearts against him, and he must have thought, *If they are ever to know what I am really like, maybe the only way is to let them eat me!*

This puts John 10 in a new perspective, doesn't it? You'll recall that Jesus was in the vicinity of Jerusalem, talking to the priests of that city. The priests had always considered themselves the "shepherds" of Israel, but Jesus said, "I am the Good Shepherd" (John 10:14). Now let me tell you the difference between the Good Shepherd and other shepherds. Shepherds normally keep sheep so that they can eat them and wear their wool. Otherwise, shepherds keep sheep to sell them, so that someone else can eat and wear them. But the Good Shepherd "lays down his life for his sheep" (v. 14). Suddenly, we realize with chilling clarity what Jesus was saying: The Good Shepherd keeps his sheep so that they can devour him!

At the Last Supper, he said, "Take, eat; this is my body.... Drink from [this cup], all of you; for this is my blood of the covenant, which is poured out for many for the forgiveness of sins" (Matt. 26:26-27). So the central ceremony of the Christian church is the taking of bread and wine as the symbols of his body and blood. We consume him in symbolism. He gave his life so that it could become ours. He shed his blood so that we could be clothed in his righteousness.

The Triumphal Procession

I recently came across a doctoral dissertation for the University of Tübingen, written by Scott Hasemann, on the theme of suffering in the gospel. Hasemann used 2 Corinthians 2:14-17 as the centerpiece for his study. That passage says:

> But thanks be to God, who in Christ always leads in triumphal procession, and through us spreads in every place the fragrance that comes from knowing him. For we are the aroma of Christ to God among those who are being saved and among those who are perishing....

The Greek word translated as "triumphal" in the phrase, "triumphal procession," is *thriambeuō*, which occurs only twice in the New Testament.[1] We have traditionally assumed that the phrase depicts a Roman general, returning from his conquests. He rides his chariot into the city triumphantly, dragging his captives behind him in their chains.

But Hasemann says the word *thriambeuō* has a distinctly different origin. It began as an Etruscan word, and the Etruscan triumphal procession went in reverse order from those of Rome. When the conquering Etruscan general or king returned from his wars, he tried to bring back the enemy king alive, in order to show him off. The conquered enemy king led the procession in his chains, so that the crowds could spit on him and ridicule him. Next came the captured soldiers. At the very end of the Etruscan victory parade came the conquering hero, who received the cheers and garlands of the adoring crowd.

Why is this significant? Because at the conclusion of the Etruscan triumphal procession, the prisoner king became a human sacrifice on an altar that commemorated the victory. Therefore, when 2 Corinthians says that Jesus leads the triumphal procession, it means that he is marching to his own execution. And we are following him.

This projects a dramatic image of our relationship with Christ. Read those words again: "Thanks be to God, who in Christ always leads us in triumphal procession, and through us spreads in every place the fragrance that comes from knowing him" (2 Cor. 2:14). The fragrance of Christ which we bear into the world is perfume from a broken vial, like the precious nard that a woman dispensed on Jesus' head (John 12:1ff.). Until the vessel is broken, his fragrance cannot be released.

Not even God can save, except by self-sacrifice. If that was true for Jesus, why should it not be true for you and me?

How Intercession Happens

That brought me to another thought: *The key to our salvation is always in somebody else.* If the atonement hadn't been accomplished in Jesus, there never would have been a chance for us. The key to our salvation is in One outside of ourselves; it is in Christ himself. Just what was it about Christ that made it possible for us to be saved?

The answer is simple: Because God cared more about you and me than he did about himself, our sinful circumstances changed.

Here we begin to get a glimmer of what biblical intercession is. True intercession isn't done by our mouths; true intercession is not a matter of words. True intercession takes place when one heart is more concerned about others than it is about itself.

We get several examples of this intercessory attitude in the Scriptures. You will remember that when Moses was up on the mountain, receiving the Law, he was gone so long that the Jews thought he had left them. So they said to Aaron, "Make gods for us" (Exod. 32:1). Aaron fashioned a golden calf and the people of Israel began worshiping it. God said to Moses, "I have seen this people, how stiffnecked they are. Now let me alone, so that my wrath may burn against them and I may consume them; and of you I will make a great nation" (v. 10). God told Moses to step aside because he was ready to wipe the slate clean and start all over again, as he had in Noah's day.

Moses' people were in danger of destruction, so he did not do as the Lord had commanded him. He did not leave God alone. Instead, he stepped up to God and pleaded on their behalf. In effect, he said, "Lord, remember the promises you made to Abraham and all of his descendants. Remember how far you've brought us. Remember all the troubles we've weathered together. Don't give up on us now."

Moses stood between the Holy One and sinful Israel. Their sin became his problem. Because of this courageous act, Israel gained a reprieve from the judgment of God. As a result, the Bible says, "The Lord changed his mind about the disaster that he planned to bring on his people" (v. 14).

We see a similar declaration in Romans 9, where Paul says, "I have great sorrow and unceasing anguish in my heart. For I could wish that I myself were accursed and cut off from Christ for the sake of my own people, my kindred according to the flesh" (vv. 2-3). Paul has reached the same place of concern for Israel that Moses had reached.

I think the biblical pattern for intercession—the only thing that can stop the judgment of God and give the world a chance—is when a person reaches the point where he cares more about somebody else than he does about himself. That's why everything we have talked about up to this point is so vitally important. We need to have the mind of Christ so that the world can be redeemed.

How am I going to get to the place where I care more about you than I do about myself? I'll never do that naturally, because the flesh will always manipulate my thoughts and emotions, so that I care about myself and try to protect my own interests. The only hope of my ever becoming useful to God is for that self-interest within me to be put to death. When my self-interest is crucified, God can begin to put his own compassion within my heart. And as he fills me with his Spirit, his love causes me to care more about you than I care about myself.

It's Not Your Problem, But...

A century ago, a young British missionary woman went to India. Her name was Amy Carmichael. When she got off the boat in India, she was horrified by most of the things she saw. But the thing that distressed her most was the way the temple girls were treated. You see, when a Hindu man died in India at that time, his wife would be burned on the same funeral pyre with him. That would normally leave a group of children with no parents. The boys were no problem because they were valuable economically; other relatives would take them in. But the girls were another matter. No one wanted them. So the girls would be given to the Hindu temples, where they were used as prostitutes. Amy Carmichael's heart ached for those girls. She thought, *If I can just get those girls out of the temples, I can turn their lives around.* So she started an orphanage and school for those temple girls.

Her plan did not sit well with the Hindu priests. The priests went to the Hindu businessmen and said, "You must do something to stop this foreign woman."

The Hindu businessmen went to the British businessmen and said, "One of your number is creating problems."

The British businessmen went to the British missionaries and said, "One of your missionary crowd is creating problems for us. You've got to stop her."

So Amy's British missionary colleagues came to her and said, "You've got to quit this."

"But what about the girls?" Amy asked.

"It's unfortunate, but that's not our problem."

About that time, she had been dealing with one of the temples to try to get back a girl whom they had taken from her school. She thought, *The priest in that temple is a religious man. He is bound to have some human compassion.* So she went to see the priest and ask for the girl. She said, "If you'll give her back to me, we'll educate her, prepare her, and she can do something significant for her country."

But she could tell by the stony lines in the priest's face and the steely glint in his eye that he was not about to turn the girl loose. She was a valuable source of revenue for his temple. So Amy thought, *Everybody is against me.*

She went to her room and got down on her knees beside her bed. She said, "Lord, I've done everything I could do, but it hasn't helped. I give up. It's not my problem anymore."

Amy Carmichael suddenly saw Jesus. He was kneeling, but not under an olive tree—he was kneeling under an Indian tamarind tree! She could see the tears streaming down his cheeks. He looked at her and said, "That's right, Amy. It's not your problem. It's not your burden. It's my problem and it's my burden. But I'm looking for someone who'll help me bear it."

Amy Carmichael then went back to work to try to save those girls. She was able to rescue hundreds of them from ignorance, disease, and temple prostitution.

That story has changed all of my thinking about intercessory prayer. Many times in my life, I've thought, *Kinlaw, you don't pray enough.* So I've tried to stir myself to work harder at intercessory prayer. Eventually, I would find a burden beginning to develop within me, so I would pat myself on the back and say, *Kinlaw, you're improving!* But I don't believe that anymore, not for a minute.

Apart from the Holy Spirit of God, you and I are too self-centered ever to care about anyone other than ourselves. If that burden for the lost ever stirs within us, it didn't start with us. It is the work of the Spirit of Jesus, saying, "Will you help me bear my burden?" If we say *yes* to him and take that burden into our hearts, we will find ourselves doing what Paul talked about when he spoke of entering into the very sufferings of Christ.

Since the key to each person's salvation lies in someone else, you can be sure that the key to someone's life lies within you. The only hope for that person is for you to allow Christ's burden to become your own. If you let him do that within you, you'll be thinking the way Christ thinks, because the mind of Christ is a cross. The cross is clearly a symbol of death, but it is also the most powerful symbol of life itself.

May God help us to enter into the fellowship of his suffering and become instruments of his redemption. We will never regret saying a total *yes* to him.

Endnotes

[1]The other occurrence of *thriambeuō* is found in Colossians 2:15, which is very similar to this passage.

APPENDIX

Sermon XIII:
"On Sin in Believers"

by John Wesley

"If any man be in Christ, he is a new creature" (2 Cor. 5:17).

I.

1. Is there then sin in him that is in Christ? Does sin *remain* in one that believes in him? Is there any sin in them that are born of God, or are they wholly delivered from it? Let no one imagine this to be a question of mere curiosity; or that it is of little importance whether it be determined one way or the other. Rather it is a point of the utmost moment to every serious Christian, the resolving of which very nearly concerns both his present and eternal happiness.

2. And yet I do not know that ever it was controverted in the primitive Church. Indeed there was no room for disputing concerning it, as all Christians were agreed. And so far as I have ever observed, the whole body of ancient Christians, who have left us anything in writing, declare with one voice, that even believers in Christ, till they are "strong in the Lord, and in the power of His might" [Eph. 6:10], have need to "wrestle with flesh and blood," with an evil nature as well as "with principalities and powers" [cf. Eph. 6:12].

3. And herein our own Church[1] (as indeed in most points) exactly copies after the primitive; declaring in her Ninth Article, "Orig-

inal sin is the corruption of the nature of every man, whereby man is in his own nature inclined to evil, so that the flesh lusteth contrary to the Spirit. And this infection of nature doth remain, yea, in them that are regenerated; whereby the lust of the flesh, called in Greek *phronēma sarkos*, is not subject to the law of God. And although there is no condemnation for them that believe, yet this lust hath of itself the nature of sin."

4. The same testimony is given by all other Churches, not only by the Greek and Romish Church, but by every Reformed Church in Europe, of whatever denomination. Indeed some of these seem to carry the thing too far, so describing the corruption of heart in a believer as scarce to allow that he has dominion over it, but rather is in bondage thereto; and, by this means, they hardly leave any distinction between a believer and an unbeliever.

5. To avoid this extreme, many well-meaning men, particularly those under the direction of the late Count Zinzendorf, ran into another [extreme], affirming that "all true believers are not only saved from the *dominion* of sin, but from the *being* of inward as well as outward sin, so that it no longer *remains* in them." And from them, about twenty years ago,[2] many of our countrymen imbibed the same opinion, that even the corruption of nature is *no more*, in those who believe in Christ.

6. It is true that, when the Germans[3] were pressed upon this head, they soon allowed (many of them at least) that "sin did still remain *in the flesh*, but not *in the heart* of the believer"; and, after a time, when the absurdity of this was shown, they fairly gave up the point, allowing that sin did still remain, though did not reign, in them that is born of God.

7. But the English, who had received it from them (some directly, some at second or third hand), were not so easily prevailed upon to part with a favorite opinion. And even when the generality of them were convinced that it was utterly indefensible, a few could not be persuaded to give it up, but maintain it to this day.

II.

1. For the sake of those who really fear God and desire to know "the truth as it is in Jesus" [Eph. 4:21], it may not be amiss to consider the point with calmness and impartiality. In doing this, I use indifferently the words *regenerate, justified* or *believers*, since, though they have not precisely the same meaning (the first implying an inward, actual change; the second a relative one; and the third the means whereby both the one and the other are wrought), yet they come to one and the same thing, as every one that believes is both justified and born of God.

2. By sin, I here understand inward sin—any sinful temper, passion, or affection such as pride, self-will, love of the world, in any kind or degree; such as lust, anger, peevishness, [or] any disposition contrary to the mind which was in Christ.

3. The question is not concerning *outward sin*, whether a child of God *commit sin* or no. We all agree and earnestly maintain, "he that committeth sin is of the devil" [1 John 3:8]. We agree, "Whosoever is born of God doth not commit sin" [1 John 3:9]. Neither do we inquire whether inward sin will *always* remain in the children of God, whether sin will continue in the soul as long as it continues in the body; nor yet do we inquire whether a justified person may *relapse* either into inward or outward sin. But simply this, Is a justified or regenerate man freed from *all sin* as soon as he is justified? Is there then no sin in his heart? Nor ever after, unless he fall from grace?

4. We allow that the state of a justified person is inexpressibly great and glorious. He is born again, "not of blood, nor of the will of the flesh, nor of the will of man, but of God" [John 1:13]. He is a child of God, a member of Christ, an heir of the kingdom of heaven. "The peace of God, which passeth all understanding, shall keep [his] heart and mind in Christ Jesus" [Phil. 4:7]. His very body is a "temple of the Holy Ghost" [1 Cor. 6:19] and an "habitation of God through the Spirit" [Eph. 2:22]. He is "created anew in Christ Jesus" [cf. Eph. 2:10]. He is *washed*, he is *sanctified*. And so long as he "walketh in love" [Eph. 5:2] (which he may always do), he worships

God in spirit and in truth. He keepeth the commandments of God and doeth those things that are pleasing in His sight, so exercising himself as to "have a conscience void of offence toward God, and toward men" [Acts 24:16]. And he has power both over outward and inward sin, even from the moment he is justified.

III.

1. "But was he not freed from all sin, so that there is no sin in his heart?" I cannot say this. I cannot believe it, because St. Paul says to the contrary. He is speaking to believers and describing the state of believers in general when he says, "The flesh lusteth against the Spirit, and the Spirit against the flesh: These are contrary the one to the other" (Gal. 5:17). Nothing can be more express. The Apostle here directly affirms that the flesh—evil nature—opposes the Spirit, even in believers; that even in the regenerate there are two principles, "contrary the one to the other."

2. Again, when he writes to the believers at Corinth, to those who are sanctified in Christ Jesus (1 Cor. 1:2), he says, "I, brethren, could not speak to you, as unto spiritual, but as unto carnal, as unto babes in Christ. Ye are yet carnal: For whereas there is among you envying and strife, are ye not carnal? (1 Cor. 3:1-3). Now here the Apostle speaks unto those who were unquestionably believers—whom, in the same breath, he styles his brethren in Christ—as being still, in a measure, carnal. He affirms there was envying (an evil temper) occasioning strife against them, and yet does not give the least intimation that they had lost their faith. Nay, he manifestly declares that they had not, for then they would not have been babes in Christ. And (what is most remarkable of all) he speaks of being carnal and babes in Christ as one and the same thing, plainly showing that every believer is (in a degree) carnal, while he is only a babe in Christ.

3. Indeed this grand point, that there are two contrary principles—nature and grace, the flesh and the Spirit—runs through all the Epistles of St. Paul, yea, through all the Holy Scriptures. Almost all the directions and exhortations therein are founded on this supposition, pointing at wrong tempers or practices in those who

are notwithstanding acknowledged by the inspired writers to be believers. And they are continually exhorted to fight with and conquer these, by the power of the faith which was in them.

4. And who can doubt but there was faith in the angel of the church of Ephesus,[4] when our Lord said to him, "I know thy works, and thy labor, and thy patience: Thou has patience, and for my name's sake hast labored, and hast not fainted" (Rev. 2:2-4)? But was there meantime no sin in his heart? Yea, or Christ would not have added, "Nevertheless, I have somewhat against thee, because thou hast left thy first love" [Rev. 2:4]. This was real sin which God saw in his heart, of which accordingly he is exhorted to *repent*. And yet we have no authority to say that, even then, he had no faith.

5. Nay, the angel of the church at Pergamos also is exhorted to *repent,* which implies sin, though our Lord expressly says, "Thou hast not denied my faith" (vv. 13, 16). And to the angel of the church at Sardis, he says, "Strengthen the things which remain, that are ready to die" [Rev. 3:2]. The good which remained was *ready to die*, but was not actually dead (Rev. 3:2). So there was still a spark of faith, even in him, which he is accordingly commanded to *hold fast* (v. 3).

6. Once more: When the Apostle exhorts believers to "cleanse themselves from all filthiness of flesh and spirit" (2 Cor. 7:1), he plainly teaches that those believers were not yet cleansed therefrom.

Will you answer, "he that abstains from all appearances of evil does *ipso facto* cleanse himself from all filthiness"? Not in any wise. For instance: A man reviles me. I feel resentment, which is filthiness in spirit, yet I say not a word. Here I "abstain from all appearance of evil" [1 Thess. 5:22], but this does not cleanse me from all filthiness of spirit, as I experience to my sorrow.

7. And as this position ("There is no sin in a believer, no carnal mind, no bent to backsliding.") is thus contrary to the Word of God, so it is to the experience of His children. These continually feel a heart bent to backsliding, a natural tendency to evil, a proneness to depart from God and cleave to the things of earth. They are

daily sensible of sin remaining in their heart—pride, self-will, unbelief—and of sin cleaving to all they speak and do, even their best actions and holiest duties. Yet at the same time they "know that they are of God" [1 John 5:19], they cannot doubt of it for a moment. They feel his Spirit clearly "witnessing with their spirit, that they are the children of God" [cf. Rom. 8:16]. They "rejoice in God through Christ Jesus, by whom they have now received the atonement" [cf. Rom. 5:11]. So that they are equally assured that sin is in them and that "Christ is in them the hope of glory" [cf. Col. 1:27].

8. "But can Christ be in the same heart where sin is?" Undoubtedly, He can, otherwise it never could be saved therefrom. Where the sickness is, there is the Physician,

> Carrying on his work within,
> Striving till He cast out sin.

Christ indeed cannot *reign* where sin *reigns*, neither will He *dwell* where any sin is *allowed*. But He *is* and *dwells* in the heart of every believer who is *fighting against* all sin, although it be not yet purified, according to the purification of the sanctuary.

9. It has been observed before that the opposite doctrine (that there is no sin in believers) is quite new in the church of Christ, that it was never heard of for seventeen hundred years, never till it was discovered by Count Zinzendorf. I do not remember to have seen the least intimation of it, either in any ancient or modern writer, unless perhaps in some of the wild, ranting Antinomians. And these likewise say and unsay, acknowledging there is sin *in their flesh*, although no sin *in their heart*. But whatever doctrine is *new* must be *wrong*, for the *old* religion is the only *true* one, and no doctrine can be right unless it is the very same "which was from the beginning" [1 John 1:1].

10. One argument more against this new, unscriptural doctrine may be drawn from the dreadful consequences of it. One says, "I felt anger today." Must I reply, "Then you have no faith"? Another says, "I know what you advise is good, but my will is quite averse to it." Must I tell him, "Then you are an unbeliever, under the wrath and

the curse of God"? What will be the natural consequence of this? Why, if he believes what I say, his soul will not only be grieved and wounded, but perhaps utterly destroyed, inasmuch as he will "cast away" that "confidence which hath great recompense of reward" [Heb. 10:35]. And having cast away his shield, how shall he "quench the fiery darts of the wicked one" [Eph. 6:16]? How shall he overcome the world, seeing "this is the victory that overcometh the world, even our faith" [1 John 5:4]? He stands disarmed in the midst of his enemies, open to all their assaults. What wonder, then, if he be utterly overthrown; if they take him captive at their will; yea, if he fall from one wickedness to another, and never see good anymore? I cannot, therefore, by any means receive this assertion that there is no sin in a believer from the moment he is justified. First, because it is contrary to the whole tenor of Scripture. Second, because it is contrary to the experience of the children of God. Third, because it is absolutely new, never heard of in the world till yesterday. And last, because it is naturally attended with the most fatal consequences, not only grieving those whom God hath not grieved, but perhaps dragging them into everlasting perdition.

IV.

1. However, let us give a fair hearing to the chief arguments of those who endeavor to support it. And it is, first, from Scripture they attempt to prove that there is no sin in a believer. They argue thus: "The Scripture says, Every believer is born of God, is clean, is holy, is sanctified, is pure in heart, has a new heart, is a temple of the Holy Ghost. Now, as 'that which is born of the flesh is flesh' [and] is altogether evil, so 'that which is born of the Spirit is spirit' [and] is altogether good. Again, a man cannot be clean, sanctified, holy, and at the same time unclean, unsanctified, unholy. He cannot be pure and impure, or have a new and an old heart together. Neither can his soul be unholy, while it is a temple of the Holy Ghost."

I have put this objection as strong as possible, that its full weight may appear. Let us now examine it, part by part. And, (1.) "That which is born of the Spirit is spirit, is altogether good." I allow the text, but not the comment. For the text affirms this, and no more—

that every man who is "born of the Spirit" is a spiritual man [John 3:6]. He is so. But so he may be, and yet not be altogether spiritual. The Christians at Corinth were spiritual men, else they had been no Christians at all; and yet they were not altogether spiritual. They were still in part carnal. "But they were fallen from grace." St. Paul says, No. They were even then babes in Christ [1 Cor. 3:1]. (2.) "But a man cannot be clean, sanctified, holy, and at the same time unclean, unsanctified, unholy." Indeed he may. So the Corinthians were. "Ye are washed," said the Apostle, "ye are sanctified"—namely, cleansed from "fornication, idolatry, drunkenness," and all other outward sin (1 Cor. 6:9-11)—and yet at the same time, in another sense of the word, they were unsanctified. They were not washed, not inwardly cleansed, from envy, evil surmising, partiality. "But sure, they had not a new heart and an old heart together." It is most sure they had; for at that very time, their hearts were *truly*, yet not *entirely*, renewed. Their carnal mind was nailed to the cross, yet it was not wholly destroyed. "But could they be unholy while they were 'temples of the Holy Ghost'?" Yes. That they were temples of the Holy Ghost is certain (1 Cor. 6:19) and it is equally certain that they were, in some degree, carnal—that is, unholy.

2. "However, there is one scripture more which will put the matter out of question: 'If any man be a believer in Christ, he is a new creature. Old things are passed away; behold, all things are become new' (2 Cor. 5:17). Now certainly a man cannot be a new creature and an old creature at once." Yes, he may. He may be partly renewed, which was the very case of those at Corinth. They were doubtless "renewed in the spirit of their mind" [Eph. 4:23], or they could not have been so much as "babes in Christ" [1 Cor. 3:1]; yet they had not the whole mind which was in Christ, for they *envied* one another. "But it is said expressly, 'Old things are passed away: All things are become new.'" But we must not so interpret the Apostle's words as to make him contradict himself. And if we will make him consistent with himself, the plain meaning of his words is this: his old judgment concerning justification, holiness, happiness, indeed con-

cerning the things of God in general, is now passed away. So are his old desires, designs, affections, tempers, and conversations. All these are undeniably become new, greatly changed from what they were; and yet, though they are new, they are not wholly new. Still he feels—to his sorrow and shame—remains of the old man, too manifest taints of his former tempers and affections, though they cannot gain any advantage over him, as long as he watches unto prayer.

3. This whole argument—"If he is clean, he is clean"; "If he is holy, he is holy"; (and twenty more expressions of the same kind may easily be heaped together)—is really no better than playing upon words. It is the fallacy of arguing from a *particular* to a *general*, of inferring a general conclusion from particular premises. Propose the sentence entire, and it runs thus: "If he is holy *at all*, he is holy *altogether*." That does not follow. Every babe in Christ is holy, and yet not altogether so. He is saved from sin, yet not entirely. [Sin] *remains*, though it does not *reign*. If you think it does not *remain* (in babes at least, whatever be the case with young men or fathers[5]), you certainly have not considered the height and depth and length and breadth of the law of God (even the law of love, laid down by St. Paul in the thirteenth of Corinthians), and that every *anomia*, disconformity to, or deviation from, this law *is sin*. Now is there disconformity to this in the heart or life of a believer? What may be in an adult Christian is another question; but what a stranger must he be to human nature, who can possibly imagine that this is the case with every babe in Christ!

4. "But believers walk after the Spirit (Rom. 8:1) and the Spirit of God dwells in them; consequently, they are delivered from the guilt, the power, or in one word, the being of sin."[6]

These are coupled together, as if they were the same thing. But they are not the same thing. The *guilt* is one thing, the *power* another, and the *being* yet another. That believers are delivered from the *guilt* and *power* of sin, we allow; that they are delivered from the *being* of it, we deny. Nor does it in any wise follow from these texts. A man may have the Spirit of God dwelling in him and may "walk in the Spirit" [Gal. 5:16], though he still feels "the flesh lusting against the Spirit" [Gal. 5:17].

5. "But 'the church is the body of Christ' (Col. 1:24); this implies that its members are washed from all filthiness. Otherwise it would follow that Christ and Belial are incorporated with each other."

Nay, it will not follow from hence—"Those who are the mystical body of Christ, still feel the flesh lusting against the Spirit."— that Christ has any fellowship with the Devil or with that sin which He enables them to resist and overcome.

6. "But are not Christians 'come to the heavenly Jerusalem,' where 'nothing defiled can enter' (Heb. 12:22)?" Yes, "and to an innumerable company of angels,...and to the spirits of just men made perfect" [Heb. 12:22-23], that is,

> Earth and heaven all agree;
> All is one great family.

And they are likewise holy and undefiled while they "walk after the Spirit," although sensible here is another principle in them, and that "these are contrary to each other" [Gal. 5:17].

7. "But Christians are reconciled to God. Now this could not be, if any of the carnal mind remained; for this is enmity against God. Consequently, no reconciliation can be effected, but by its total destruction."

We are "reconciled to God through the blood of the cross" [cf. Col. 1:20]. And in that moment the *phronēma sarkos*, the corruption of nature, which is enmity with God, is put under our feet. The flesh has no more dominion over us. But it still *exists*, and it is still in its natural enmity with God, lusting against his Spirit.

8. "But 'they that are Christ's have crucified the flesh, with its affections and lusts' (Gal. 5:24)." They have so; yet it remains in them still and often struggles to break from the cross. "Nay, but they have 'put off the old man with his deeds' (Col. 3:9)." They have. And, in the sense above described, "old things have passed away; all things are become new" [2 Cor. 5:17]. A hundred texts may be cited to the same effect; and they will all admit of the same answer. "But, to say all in one word, 'Christ gave himself for the church, that

it might be holy, and without blemish' (Eph. 5:25, 27)." And so it will be in the end. But it never was yet, from the beginning to this day.

9. "But let experience speak: All who are justified do at that time find an absolute freedom from all sin." That I doubt. But if they do, do they find it ever after? Else you gain nothing. "If they do not, it is their own fault." That remains to be proved.

10. "But in the very nature of things, can a man have pride in him, and not be proud? Anger, and yet not be angry?"

A man may have *pride* in him, may think of himself in some particulars above what he ought to think (and so be proud in that particular), and yet not be a proud man in his general character. He may have *anger* in him, yea, and a strong propensity to furious anger without *giving way* to it. "But can anger and pride be in that heart, where only meekness and humility are felt?" No, but *some* pride and anger may be in that heart where there is much humility and meekness.

"It avails not to say, These tempers are there, but they do not reign. For sin cannot, in any kind or degree, exist where it does not reign; for *guilt* and *power* are essential properties of sin. Therefore, where one of them is, all must be."

Strange indeed! "Sin cannot, in any kind or degree, *exist* where it does not *reign*"? Absolutely contrary to this [is] to all experience, all Scripture, all common sense. Resentment of an affront is sin; it is *anomia*, disconformity to the law of love. This has existed in me a thousand times. Yet it did not, and does not, *reign*. "But *guilt* and *power* are essential properties of sin; therefore, where one is, all must be." No. In the instance before us, if the resentment I feel is not yielded to, even for a moment, there is no guilt at all, no condemnation from God upon that account. And in this case, it has no *power*. Though it "lusteth against the Spirit," it cannot prevail. Here, therefore, as in ten thousand instances, there is *sin* without either *guilt* or *power*.

11. "But the supposing sin in a believer is pregnant with every thing frightening and discouraging. It implies the contending with

a power that has the possession of our strength, maintains his usurpation of our hearts, and there prosecutes the war in defiance of our Redeemer." Not so. The supposing sin is in us does not imply that it has the possession of our strength, no more than a man crucified has the possession of those who crucify him. As little does it imply that "sin maintains its usurpation of our hearts." The usurper is dethroned. He remains indeed where he once reigned, but remains *in chains.* So that he does, in some sense, "prosecute the war," yet he grows weaker and weaker while the believer goes on from strength to strength, conquering and to conquer.

12. "I am not satisfied yet: he that has sin in him is a slave to sin. Therefore, you suppose a man to be justified, while he is a slave to sin. Now if you allow men may be justified while they have pride, anger, or unbelief in them—nay, if you aver these are (at least for a time) in all that are justified—what wonder that we have so many proud, angry, unbelieving believers?"

I do not suppose any man who is justified is a slave to sin. Yet I do suppose sin remains (at least for a time) in all that are justified.

"But if sin remains in a believer, he is a sinful man. If pride, for instance, then he is proud; if self-will, then he is self-willed; if unbelief, then he is an unbeliever, consequently no believer at all. How then does he differ from unbelievers, from unregenerate men?" This is still mere playing upon words. It means no more than, if there is sin, pride, self-will in him, then—there is sin, pride, and self-will. And this nobody can deny. In that sense, then, he is proud or self-willed. But he is not proud or self-willed in the same sense that unbelievers are, that is, *governed* by pride or self-will. Herein he differs from unregenerate men. They *obey* sin; he does not. Flesh is in them both, but they "walk after the flesh," he "walks after the Spirit."

"But how can *unbelief* be in a believer?" That word has two meanings. It means either no faith or little faith, either the *absence* of faith or the *weakness* of it. In the former sense, unbelief is not in a believer; in the latter, it is in all babes. Their faith is commonly mixed with doubt or fear—that is, in the latter sense, with unbelief. "Why are ye fearful," says our Lord, "O ye of little faith?" [Matt. 8:20]. Again, "O thou of little faith, wherefore didst thou doubt?" [Matt. 14:31]. You see here was *unbelief* in *believers*, little faith and much unbelief.

13. "But this doctrine that sin remains in believers, that a man may be in the favor of God while he has sin in his heart, certainly tends to encourage men in sin." Understand the proposition right, and no such consequence follows. A man may be in God's favor though he feel sin, but not if he *yields* to it. *Having sin* does not forfeit the favor of God; *giving way to sin* does. Though the flesh in you "lust against the Spirit," you may still be a child of God. But if you "walk after the flesh," you are a child of the Devil. Now this doctrine does not encourage to *obey* sin, but to resist it with all our might.

V.

1. The sum of all is this: There are in every person, even after he is justified, two contrary principles—nature and grace—termed by St. Paul, the *flesh* and the *Spirit*. Hence, even though babes in Christ are *sanctified*, yet it is only in part. In a degree according to the measure of their faith, they are spiritual; yet in a degree, they are carnal. Accordingly, believers are continually exhorted to watch against the flesh, as well as the world and the Devil. And to this agrees the constant experience of the children of God. While they feel this witness in themselves, they feel a will not wholly resigned to the will of God. They know they are in him, and yet find a heart ready to depart from him, a proneness to evil in many instances and a backwardness to that which is good. The contrary doctrine is wholly new, never heard of in the church of Christ from the beginning of his coming into the world till the time of Count Zinzendorf; and it is attended with the most fatal consequences. It cuts off all watching against our evil nature, against the Delilah which we are told is gone, though she is still lying in our bosom. It tears away the shield of weak believers, deprives them of their faith and so leaves them exposed to all assaults of the world, the flesh, and the Devil.

2. Let us therefore hold fast the sound doctrine "once delivered to the saints" [Jude 3] and delivered down by them, with the written Word, to all succeeding generations: That although we are renewed, cleansed, purified, sanctified the moment we truly believe in Christ, yet we are not then renewed, cleansed, purified altogether; but the flesh, the evil nature, still remains (though subdued) and wars against the Spirit. So much the more let us use all diligence in "fighting the good fight of faith" [1 Tim. 6:12]. So much the more earnestly let us "watch and pray" against the enemy within [Matt. 26:40]. The more carefully let us take to ourselves and "put on the whole armor of God" [Eph. 6:11], that although "we wrestle" both "with flesh and blood, and with principalities, and powers, and wicked spirits in high places" [Eph. 6:12], we "may be able to withstand in the evil day, and having done all, to stand" [Eph. 6:13].

Endnotes

[1]That is, the Anglican Church.

[2]This sermon was first published in 1747.

[3]That is, the Moravians who studied under Count Zinzendorf.

[4]The Greek word *angelos* can be translated as "angel" or "messenger," so most Bible scholars believe the "angels" of the churches in Revelation were the pastors of those congregations.

[5]Wesley's reference to "babes," "young men," and "fathers" in Christ is an allusion to 1 John 2:12-14.

[6]Wesley's footnote: "What follows for some pages is an answer to a paper, published in the *Christian Magazine*, pp. 577-582. I am surprised Mr. Dodd should give such a paper a place in his magazine, which is directly contrary to our Ninth Article." Apparently, all of the following quotations are from the objectionable article that Wesley cites.

Index

Parables, 17, 53
Pascal, Blaise, 31
Paul, Apostle, 14, 69-72, 77, 79-80,
    82-85, 87-91, 95-96, 97n, 99-101,
    104-106, 120, 129, 132, 137
Pentecost, 19, 67, 91-93, 107
Perfection, Wesley's view of, 75-76
Peter, Apostle, 14, 17, 42, 54-55, 58-
    61, 64-68, 80, 90, 92, 99
Pharisees, 49, 56, 59
Philippi, church at, 99-100, 104-105
Philosophy, 14, 31, 87
Phroneō, 14, 70, 75
Predestination, 47
Prevenient grace, 89, 93
Pride, 9, 28, 94-95, 127, 130, 135-
    136

Reason, inadequacy of, 28
Rebellion, 18, 62, 73, 103-104, 106,
    133
Redemption, 22, 25, 41, 43-44, 46,
    52, 57, 84-86, 93, 101, 123
Reformed theology, 25, 126
Regeneration, 23, 94
Relationships, theology shaped by,
    66
Resentment, 45, 102, 106, 129, 135
Righteousness, forensic, 85
Roseveare, Helen, 103, 105

Sabbath, 56
Saints, 79-80, 90, 138
Salvation, 115, 123
Sanctification, 8, 34, 36, 84-86, 94,
    137
Sarai/Sarah, 15, 24-25, 28, 33
Saul, King, 15
Sayers, Dorothy, 42
Scriptures, purpose of, 7, 9, 12
Self-adequacy, 62

Self-interest, 23
Self-renunciation, 104
Self-sacrifice, 115, 118
Signs and wonders, 68n
Simpson, A. B., 91, 97
Sin, 23, 26, 33; in believers, 125;
    Wesley's definition of, 127, 137
Smith, Hannah Whitall, 32, 85
Social gospel, 101
Solomon, King, 17
Status, 63, 65, 67, 76, 102

Temple, William, 27
Thambeō, 64
Thriambeuō, 118, 123
Transfiguration, Mount of, 18, 61,
    80
Trinity, 26, 35
Tson, Josef, 108-109, 116

Unbelief, 28, 94-95, 130, 136-137
Universalism, 47

Watchfulness, 31, 38, 94, 133, 137-
    138
Welch, Reuben, 32
Wesley, John, 65, 75, 89, 93, 97, 101,
    125
Wesley, Charles, 39
Wesleyan theology, 47, 101

Zinzendorf, Count Nicholas, 126,
    130, 137-138